REVIEWS

We are all trying to survive during this time of uncertainty and instability. "Piloting Through Chaos" elucidates the path. Julian Gresser's brilliant blending of Eastern philosophy and Western intellect, classic stories and personal experiences is masterful! His insightful process enables us to remember who we are, most importantly, but then to determine where we are and what we want. So whether we are negotiating with our teenage son about his curfew or with a multinational about a merger, the basic steps, The Five Rings, will show us the way. The market is flooded with books and tapes about negotiating . . . but no one, until now, offers insight into the underlying essence of our interpersonal abilities. This fresh approach, if followed, can be transformative for us as individuals, and as a nation.

—*Claudine Schneider*
Former U.S. Congresswoman

Julian Gresser's work shows with insight, style and imagination how integrity, that most fundamental of human virtues, continues to be vital to success, and even survival, in the ongoing negotiation of life in our rapidly changing world. The added value in *Piloting Through Chaos* is the author's suggestions on how integrity can be cultivated by conscious thought and action, and on how core integrity can affect outcomes in a variety of contexts.

—*Peter L. Murray*
Visiting Professor of Law
Harvard Law School

Julian Gresser's book reminds me of the title of a book by the Danish philosopher Søren Kirkegaard,"Purity of Heart Is to Will One Thing." Our usual state is to will different things with different parts of ourselves—typified by the conflict between "desire" and "conscience." Gresser has made a powerful case for the development of integrated will, of "integrity" as a sense of connectedness, coherence, wholeness and vitality. His familiarity with Oriental culture makes this book an extremely penetrating and valuable tool. It is delightful to read, and full of deep wisdom.

—*Willis Harman*
President, Institute of Noetic Sciences

JULIAN GRESSER is an international attorney, negotiator, consultant, author and inventor. From 1976-83 Mr. Gresser was twice Visiting Mitsubishi Professor at the Harvard Law School and also taught seminars on technology, economics and law as a Visiting Professor at MIT. He has been a consultant to the U.S. State Department, the Prime Minister's Office of Japan, the World Bank, the Republic of Korea, the People's Republic of China and the European Commission, as well as hundreds of U.S., European and Japanese companies. Mr. Gresser is the author of two other books, *Environmental Law in Japan* (MIT Press, 1981) and *Partners in Prosperity: Strategic Industries in the U.S. and Japan* (McGraw Hill, 1984), as well as numerous professional articles on technology, economics, and law. His company, Lōgōs Networks Corporation, has developed a new way of automating the ongoing training and coaching of negotiating, marketing, sales, and project development teams in the field.

Piloting Through Chaos

Wise Leadership • Effective Negotiation

For the 21st Century

Julian Gresser

Five Rings Press
A Division of Lōgōs Networks Corporation
P.O. Box 720
Sausalito, CA 94965

General/Training: 415-331-7212
Fax: 415-331-5264
Tech.Support: 510-527-7970 (same for fax)
E-Mail: integrity@logosnet.com
BBS: 510-527-7439

First Edition
Printed in the United States of America on acid-free paper
distributed in the United States by Lōgōs Networks Corporation
and JG Enterprises

Library of Congress Catalog Card No. 95-062030

Library of Congress Cataloging-in-Publication Data
Gresser, Julian, 1943
PILOTING THROUGH CHAOS
Wise Leadership · Effective Negotiation for the 21st Century

Includes bibliography and index

Julian Gresser—1st ed.
        p. cm.
  ISBN 1-888278-00-5 (alk. paper)

Cover design by Windgate Press, Sausalito, California

Integrity Series. Volume I

For all those who strive
To turn the Wheel for better.

ACKNOWLEDGEMENTS

With much gratitude I acknowledge these friends and colleagues who, like the tides, currents, and beneficial breezes have helped to push this small craft forward: my dear wife, Angela, inspiring Muse, loyal friend, helpful critic, gentle hand—at the crests and through the valleys; Dr. John Tarrant, who first introduced me to the principle of integrity, for his thoughtful and wise advice—was there ever a better teacher, counselor and friend? Dr. Elmer Green, who introduced me to the mysteries of the "inner-outer" dialogue when we first began our collaboration in 1987, for his many good suggestions. Noelle Oxenhandler, descending at a late stage like some benevolent Fury, who shook the best out of the manuscript and me; Gisela Kahn Gresser for her generous financial support, an act of true friendship at a critical stage; Dr. Jeffrey Mishlove, Paula Fox, Tod Brannan and Oliver Oldman for their useful comments on earlier drafts and also Linda and Wayne Bonnett of Windgate Press who designed the cover of this book and have been such good consultants during its production. Lastly, I thank my loyal assistant, Mary Jane Phelps, and her staff at Sea Cliff Secretarial, in particular Harriet March Page, for their unflagging support and cheer through months of endless "final" drafts.

CONTENTS

AUTHOR'S PREFACE   viii

THE READER'S COMPASS   xiv

I.   INTEGRITY IN ACTION   1

II.   THE FIVE RINGS   19

III.   LIGHT AND SHADOW   57

IV.   HOW TO PRACTICE   110

V.   THE LŌGŌS NETWORK   131

GLOSSARY   147

BIBLIOGRAPHY   154

INDEX   157

CONTINUING YOUR PRACTICE   160

PREFACE

If you were flying the friendly skies on #101 bound from New York to Los Angeles, conceivably it might matter to you that:

- The pilot is not insane.
- The plane has a specific direction so that you don't change course every 15 minutes.
- #101 is well-built and won't fall apart over the Rockies.
- Reliable instruments are on board in case you hit rough weather.

Suppose you could have the same sturdy navigational system in your business or personal life? At any time under all conditions you could instantly assess:

- Where you are
- Where you want to be
- How to get there
- How to adjust to change
- How to correct errors
- How to repeat successes
- What moves to make next

That's my purpose in writing this book: to give you the **Pilot's Compass.**

I came upon this "navigation system" in a curious way. In the early 1980s I moved to Tokyo and opened a law firm. In my business dealings there I faced some of the world's most financially powerful, resourceful and cunning negotiators. I began to ask myself these questions: How is it that some of the smartest, most effective American and European managers behave in their Japanese dealings like deer caught in a car's headlight? Why is it that virtually every European and American company operating in Japan is hostage to its Japanese management? As the months passed, I made two interesting discoveries.

First, I discovered that a large number of Japanese corporate teams and the Japanese government itself were deploying a largely hidden (even from themselves!), culturally-embedded system of navigation. This system comprises at least a hundred moves which cause havoc within the decision-making process of their opponents, foreign as well as Japanese, by attacking its core "integrity."

Second, I concluded that the antidote lay not in casting blame or finding fault, but rather in helping my clients focus on what they could actually manage—specifically, redeeming and rebuilding their compromised "integrity." I began to counsel my American and European clients in this way, and even some Japanese clients in their negotiations with other Japanese, and I soon found that once they understood and could predict the moves under the "code," they managed very well.

As I say, the key to my discoveries was integrity. It is such an old-fashioned word—even schoolmarmish or boy scoutish—who would suspect what revolutionary possibilities it conceals? But the more I have looked inside and around this word, the more it began to reveal a mysterious and dynamic power.

What is this **power?**

Integrity is the capacity of every human being, indeed of any living system, to remain connected, coherent, whole, and adaptively alive. It can be understood on several levels:

- **First**, it is a state of being. **You know** when you are in the state, and you know when it has been compromised.
- **Second**, integrity is a principle of ethical and conscious action. Ethics flows from consciousness. When a person has **integrity** his or her actions will naturally be ethical ones.
- **Third**, integrity is a principle for corporate and societal organization. Companies and enterprises of every kind that build integrity will be those that are profitable, well run, and happy.
- **Fourth**, integrity is a standard for policy making. In the area of environmental law, for example, integrity analysis offers a new way to reconcile conflicts and discrepancies among air, water, land use, endangered species and a host of other protective laws and regulations.
- **Fifth**, integrity is a force of nature. If entropy is the power

in the physical realm that pulls things apart and wears them down, integrity is the countervailing force that valiantly stands up to entropy and keeps us whole, joyous and alive.

In integrity, I found the cornerstone of a new theoretical and practical approach to navigation in the world.

I should explain how my concept of "navigation" based on integrity differs from conventional notions of negotiation. Navigation is broader and includes intelligent and wise decision making, character and effective action. This distinction has critical and practical implications, particularly for the popular so-called "win-win" school of negotiation.

- **First,** as a way of bypassing positional bargaining and resolving some kinds of disputes, the "win-win" model has made important contributions. But as a system of navigation I have found it overly concerned with the result, too in need of resolution (agreement) and not willing enough to accept, indeed to enjoy, the process. And this flaw, I have found, is very dangerous, because it entirely misses the fact, so evident to me in my own Japanese dealings, that the negotiation—the navigation process—is continuing and unending. In Japanese negotiations there is always another river to ford or a new mountain to climb, and one is never out of the game.

- **Second,** the prevailing "win-win" school places far too much emphasis on strategies and tactics and too little on the development of character from which all sound tactics I believe must spring. And this unwillingness to address the basic and hard issues of changing habits and behaviors is also a critical failing. In my work in the United States, Japan and other countries the model did not prepare me adequately to deal with the shadow— the duplicity, treachery, stupidity and cruelty swirling around the world. Only character, I have come to see, can hold the ship together in the face of these.

- **Third,** because the "win-win" model is not rooted enough in the ooze of life, because it steps back from and will not come to grips with darkness and turbulence, it also fails to see the light. Too sheltered and cloistered, it does not understand that the process of navigation itself creates countless opportunities each step of the way to develop and to transform ourselves.

Toward the end of the 1980s I began to test and put my new system into practice. I scored a number of successes during this period, including helping a San Francisco-based trading company transform its $8 million Japanese branch into a Japanese company listed on the Tokyo Over-the-Counter Exchange with a capitalized value of over $1 billion. What was most curious and paradoxical about this case was that everyone benefited: the owners, the investing public, the managers, the employees, the underwriters, even both governments, each of which claimed credit for the success. One of the great commercial "win-win" victories in the history of U.S.-Japanese commercial relations was achieved without any of the parties giving a thought to "win-win" at all! I have seen the same result in many other cases in which I have since been involved.

As my docket of cases expanded and my experience continued to develop, I soon found I had more than enough material to prepare a program of instruction featuring Japan, and based on my method of cultivating integrity, which I now call, The Five Rings. In 1991 I began to conduct training and coaching programs for teams of negotiators at leading companies in the United States, Japan and Europe, as well as at the European Commission. These programs provided me with the opportunity to refine my methodology and my ideas were very well-received. The model was still not complete, however. On a personal front I continued to struggle with the desire to embody more deeply in my own life the principles of effective action that I had worked so hard to give my clients. In this struggle I made an important discovery. I naturally assumed that integrity was the means of becoming a more effective navigator. Then suddenly one day I realized that the converse proposition was equally true: the daily negotiations I was in—even casual encounters—provided the means to fortify integrity. In other words, the process of navigation—precisely because it is so focused, practical and engaged—is itself the vehicle of transformation.

This discovery made the threads in the pattern come together and enabled me to see with fresh eyes. "Winning" and "losing" became less important. Creating value and meaning in life, becoming productive and useful to others became the focus. To work on the quality of integrity—to polish and refine it like a jewel—was in itself a great joy. No special magic was required, no special effects in the form of external stimuli or mental fantasies. For the first time in my life I found more than enough magic in the mundanity of daily transactions, meetings, confrontations, and accords.

This is not to suggest that I have become stuck, however happily, within my office walls. Quite the contrary. Like a plant putting forth tendrils, my practice of integrity has led me to see new connections among things I never saw connected before. The first connection or reconnection has been with nature. Now as I take walks in the Marin Headlands near my home, everywhere I look I can see how nature expresses and celebrates its integrity in every leaf, every stone, and in the humblest creatures.

At the same time the practice is enabling me to tap the richness of human culture in a way that seems to me radically new. Now when I encounter great works of art, literature and music, they are far more than exalted forms of entertainment. Through my practice I have begun to detect a common, underlying structure in the masterpieces of Shakespeare, Mozart and Leonardo da Vinci, and in the works of other masters, and to see that it is their perfect integrity that endows them with such force and power.

Perhaps the most interesting discovery for me is how the skill of integrity can be refined and perfected by using the latest breakthroughs in information technology. During the past two years in collaboration with Tod Brannan, an expert software designer and engineer, I have come upon a series of inventions that can be best summarized under the code name, "E-Mail from Shakespeare." Together we have developed a way to reanimate not only Shakespeare but all the great figures of history, living and dead, and not only masters of literature but also musicians, artists and creators of all kinds, and, by the computer, to invite them all to become personal advisors, friends and coaches on our most practical and pressing issues and concerns. We call our new software program, The Artful Navigator.

In sum, the cultivation of integrity has provided for me an answer to the ancient question of what it means to lead "a good life." Tested in the fire of the most practical human interactions, the practice is anchored in the deepest waters of human experience and fueled by our highest aspirations. For ultimately, the implications are global.

It does not take a prophet to see we are heading into an electric storm without a compass. Around the world each year more people go hungry, more Bosnias crop up, the living environment dies a little more, and the criers of bigotry and violence go about the streets. In the United States a new cynicism and nastiness has crept into our political life and the faith of the electorate in truthfulness and decency is breaking. At the basic level where most people live their lives, they look for assurance that things will eventually be okay. But there are no assurances in the 1990s and they feel powerless and afraid.

There is a natural tendency in this century of extraordinary technical accomplishment to believe we can solve any problem solely by our wits without our hearts also. But the tools themselves—the computer and telecommunications, for example—are not making us any wiser, and there is a fair concern among a broad section of sober-minded people that they are only breeding new forms of vulgarity and brutality, and in the end, will leave us feeling more truncated, fragmented and alone.

I see a way out that offers hope. Let us make integrity the magnetic pole of our navigation system—a common language and method of operation linking all peoples—and let us use our new tools—multimedia, the Internet, perhaps someday a Wisdom SuperHighway—to help us discover new and better ways to think and learn and get on together. It is to this special goal that this book is dedicated.

Julian Gresser
Sausalito, California

THE READER'S COMPASS

In writing this book I have in mind two large groups of readers. The first are people in business who seek to become more effective, but who will understand that one key is learning how to find greater joy, meaning, and satisfaction in the work itself. This broad group includes senior and middle managers, lawyers, physicians, architects, designers, teachers and other professionals, and tradespeople of all kinds. It includes environmentalists, political and social activists and other reformers who are looking for a more practical means to move their cause robustly forward; and also new leaders at the national and local levels who today are searching for a fresh outlook, a new vocabulary, and a better way to solve the country's problems.

The second group encompasses other persons not in business who have chosen a spiritual path or an artistic one, who have in some sense removed themselves from the world of affairs, but who still want to make a useful contribution and don't quite know how; and also those who lack a practical method to maneuver when their feet are in the fire.

In its organization, the book is straightforward and practical and is designed to help you quickly grasp the elements of the method and then to serve as a reference. Chapter I introduces the book's concept of integrity through an initial case study. Chapter II begins with the importance of clarity of vision and a mission of service and then goes on to develop the basics of The Five Rings. Chapter III is concerned with more advanced skills and powers that come through the steady cultivation of integrity. Chapter IV offers a simple program of practice. Chapter V explores how The Five Rings can provide a common language and system of navigation for large numbers of players around the world interlinked by the Internet and other new networks of communication.

Whenever possible I have illustrated the key principles and moves by cases and stories which will enable you to learn vicariously and by example. Many of these cases are drawn from my own professional experience, but some are ancient stories and there are many classical references. This also is part of the method, because I want to show the richness and interconnection of things that are at once timely and timeless.

For this reason also the book is written in the form of an imaginary dialogue with Tod Brannan and his wife and colleague, Paula Fox. In Greek the original meaning of "dialogue" was "through" (dia) "lōgōs" or reason. A dialogue was a discourse on the theme of sanity and good judgment. My purpose is to open a dialogue with my readers, and to extend the first threads which you can then weave closely and usefully into the patterns of your own life.

Socrates' Prayer:

> *Beloved Pan, and all ye other gods who haunt this place,*
> *Grant me the beauty of the inward spirit*
> *And may the outer and inner man be as one.*

—Phaedrus

I. INTEGRITY IN ACTION

"The dragon fly
perches on the stick
raised to strike him."

—Basho

"In combat if you know where to move you are
already too late! The opportunity is lost. You must
feel it and act before you have knowledge of it."

—A martial artist

"All things are ready, if our minds be so."

—Shakespeare - Henry V

"Those who can change are free."

— The Artful Navigator

I. INTEGRITY IN ACTION

I met him for the first time in his office on Route 128 near Boston. Let's call him Flanagan. He was the president of a small, struggling electronics company. Although he was a brilliant physicist and an engineer, he found himself over his head in a negotiation with one of the giant Japanese conglomerates. For months he had gotten nowhere, and he had this awful sense that his company's precious know-how—its only asset of real value -through unwitting disclosures by him and his staff, was leaking from his company like a sieve.

Soon after, Flanagan joined a "pool" of executives who were training with me over months to become more effective in their Japanese negotiations. He approached the training with the same dedication—the same curiosity of mind—with which he approached the design and engineering of a new integrated circuit. But then I lost touch with him for about a year after the program ended.

"How is Flanagan doing?" I asked an acquaintance one day who knew him well. "Haven't you heard?" he responded. "He's had a sensational success. The Japanese have invested over ten million dollars in his company, and the venture capitalists on his board can't believe it. "How did he do it?" I asked. "The last I heard he was floundering."

"You should call him and find out yourself," my friend replied.

So I did. Flanagan and I met for dinner at a Japanese restaurant in Boston. He looked years younger. He had a hard, life-tested quality that was very pleasing. This was the story Flanagan told me with a twinkle in his eye.

FLANAGAN'S STORY

"I arrived in Tokyo foolishly unaccompanied by my chief lieutenant or even a reliable translator (I don't think I'll do that again). Anyway on the way to our meeting—I had come for the signing ceremony for our 'technology joint venture'—my host, who was sitting in the taxi beside me, passed me an envelope. 'It's the final draft,' he said, smiling, and then returned to looking blankly out the window at the coffee shops, sushi bars, pachinko parlors, and crowds that were already bustling to their jobs at 8:30 on this Monday morning. I scarcely bothered to look at what was inside the envelope, as I and my lawyers had already reviewed every word and every nuance in the text of this agreement a hundred times. 'Enough,' I said. 'If I can't trust these people now, I never will.'

"But then I got this feeling—call it intuition—that I ought at least to have a look. I opened the envelope and began to scan the text. What a surprise! A different deal. I couldn't believe my eyes. 'What is this?' I began to stammer to my Japanese host. But by this time we had arrived at our meeting place, somewhere on the 13th floor of a large grey building in the Marunouchi area of Tokyo. We got off at the 21st floor and I was escorted past lines of pretty bowing girls and attendants to a waiting room with immaculate white doilies on the arm rests of leather chairs, and from there into a large conference room where thirteen Japanese executives rose in unison exactly in attention as I entered the room. My ordeal had begun."

"What did you do?" I asked.

"What could I do?" he continued. "The first thing I did was panic. What does one say or do in such a situation? I felt like bounding right out of the room shrieking. Now that might have been an interesting tactic! But instead I got a grip and remembered our training, settled down, and decided to have some fun.

"I needed time to regain my bearings, so I resolved not to understand anything. Even if I did understand, not to let on, and to let them do all the talking, all the explaining, while I struggled to grasp their meaning. I wanted them to expend some of their time and effort, and get involved in trying to help me understand, while I figured out what to do. Actually having no translator along helped my strategy.

"So that's how we spent the whole day, the thirteen executives earnestly explaining, I earnestly trying to understand
and never quite catching on. Then we adjourned. Everyone was tired, but they were more exhausted than I. I was
beginning to find my second wind.

"The next morning we reconvened. I was greeted with a
slight nod and a grunt or two—a glimmer of recognition
by some of the thirteen executives, who sat exactly in the
same positions as they had the day before. An attendant
brought in some black coffee. Otherwise no one moved.
There was only silence." Flanagan poured himself a cup
of sake and watched for my reaction.

"Silence?" I repeated. (I have seen such situations before,
and they usually take odd turns.)

"Utter silence."

"For how long?"

"First five minutes, then ten, fifteen maybe. No one said a
word." Flanagan's eyes were sparkling in delight. "I got up,
poured myself some coffee, because I'd be damned if I
would be the first to speak. I just planted my feet and held
on.

"About 20 minutes later, they couldn't stand it any longer.
'Dr. Flanagan, what did you think of our proposal?' their
spokesman blurted out. 'We spent all day yesterday discussing it with you. Surely you must have an opinion.'

"'Frankly, I'm very disappointed,' I said. 'I appreciate very
much all the time you have spent in explaining your ideas
to me, but actually this is not why I came to Tokyo. This is
not the deal we have been discussing for months, on which
we agreed three weeks ago in Boston. I'm going home.
Please call a taxi.'

"'Dr. Flanagan,' the lead man rose from his seat. 'This is a great mistake, a cultural misunderstanding.'

"'I must,' I said. 'Please ask your assistant to call me a taxi. I have checked and there is a United Airlines flight leaving Narita at 5:30 p.m. I don't want to be late.'

"'You can't go! There's a misunderstanding!'

"'Kindly call me a taxi. I'm going home,' I said in a level voice."

"So that's what I did." He took a long swig of sake and smiled at me.

"Very good, very good," I exclaimed, sensing the momentum building in his story. "But what did you do next?"

"Nothing. I did absolutely nothing. They sent me a stream of faxes that week and the next, but I did not respond to them. I waited to think things over, get my bearings, and sort out what I really wanted from them."

"What happened then?"

"Finally, I replied to their faxes and told them I was prepared to discuss the original transaction, but no more games. Do you know, they canceled their vacations and came to visit us, and then things got back on track. There were a few other ups and downs, right up to the end. They tried to squeeze a few additional concessions by telling me that the president of their parent company, a multibillion dollar conglomerate, had committed to come to the signing ceremony, and unless I signed on the terms they wanted, the meeting would have to be canceled. This would be embarrassing since everything had been arranged. But I saw no reason to give in, and I told them so. And then they dropped these last conditions."

"How have things worked out?"

"Marvelously. They gave us everything we asked for and more. Under our arrangement we have committed to train several of their people and we have honored every promise we made. I have taken a personal interest in seeing that the engineers and their families are well cared for. They have learned from us and we are learning from them. And now we are discussing the next phase of the project. Somehow our silent confrontation in Tokyo put things back on track. It's as if we gave them a sense of who we are—of boundaries—which actually was comforting to them. We both gained room to breathe and to respect each other a little better."

Brannan: In a nutshell, Julian, what is the central lesson of this case?

Gresser: Trainability—the ability to adjust instantly and creatively, especially in unpredictable and surprising situations. In this sense the different attitudes and peculiar practices of business in Japan (at least from Western eyes) present wonderful opportunities to develop this skill. Flanagan could have let his fear and panic overwhelm him. But he possessed that intangible quality of character— I call it *gravitas* or weightedness—to hold on. And from this place of self-containment came a sense of play. The game was serious but he had a taste for the hunt.

Brannan: What is the relationship of trainability to chaos—the central theme of this discourse?

Gresser: We have been taught to believe we have no control over the chaos in our lives. Like the fates chaos is simply here and we are stuck. In our need for certainty and order, we see chaos as an aberration and are surprised when it suddenly appears. But chaos is always with us. Flanagan's story introduces the idea that there is also almost always negotiating room, a path. Trainability is the ability to discover the path.

Brannan: You say that trainability is a quality of character. What then is the relationship of character to chaos?

Gresser: The Greek philosopher Herakleitos wrote over two thousand years ago, "Character is destiny." This idea is even encrypted in the original meaning of the Greek word for character, *charattein*, "to engrave." Thus by our own hand we imprint our unique story on the tablets of our life. The same idea is contained in the *I Ching* and in most of the other great books of wisdom. We have far more leverage over the "external" fates than we even dreamed possible, and the beginning of this realization is when we gain dominion over ourselves.

CHAOS AND CHARACTER

Flanagan's story makes this point: Strategy and tactics are useful but they are insufficient. To deal effectively with the upheavals, the great issues in life, as they step out of the void called "chaos," tactics must be built upon a foundation of character. In this respect it seems to me much of the contemporary writing on negotiation is deficient. There is too much stress on strategic "moves" and too little emphasis on the deeper character work which is so essential in the difficult times of the 1990s. That is why this narrative is subtitled, *Wise Leadership • Effective Negotiation*, because these two are inseparably entwined, especially if we include within the definition of "leadership" the most basic of all abilities, which is the ability to lead oneself.

Our great epic heroes confirm this point. Odysseus was not only a master strategist he was also a superior man (the Greek word is *aristos*). Tactics were important, but in the end it was force of character and a keen intelligence that brought him safely home to Ithaca.

Brannan:

What is the essential quality that enabled Flanagan to adjust so adroitly? Is there an algorithm to the method that anyone, not only kings and epic heroes, can grasp easily?

Gresser:

INTEGRITY AS A PRINCIPLE OF NATURE

There is. I call it "integrity." By integrity, I mean a sense of connectedness, coherence, wholeness and vitality. Integrity is the capacity of every living thing to maintain its hold in the face of entropy, disorder and uncertainty, its link to the living world, its ability to carry on its life, however humble. Take the smallest, simplest creature—a paramecium, for example—and you will see integrity in action! Surround this little fellow with a toxic substance, and he will fight to hold integrity, the right—if one can use this word about so humble a creature—to be whole and to continue its existence. The paramecium understands integrity very well.

THE PHYSICAL EXPRESSION OF INTEGRITY

Tod, integrity is a physical experience, not only a theoretical principle. You **know** when you have integrity. You can feel it in your joints. You feel it as you breathe, you can feel it in your heart. If I attach a thermistor to your finger, you will have an objective way to gauge the degree of your body's integrity. If you become suddenly frightened—in other words, disconnected from the source of your own vitality—the temperature in your finger will fall and there will be many other changes in key indicators—for example, staggered breathing, rapid heart rate, hormonal changes, changes in brain waves and so forth. Your integrity will be momentarily compromised. If the fear persists, gradually you will lose the connection to your power source. (This is precisely what happens in a state of **panic** which contains the root meaning of "everywhere." In panic your consciousness is widely dispersed and without a center.) On the other hand, when you are at ease and have a sense of time to spare, when you feel, as I am sure you often have, abundant and vital, the temperature will rise in your fingers, perhaps to 96°. At such times you have a sense of "just being" in the flow, especially in action, and of a brighter, happier world growing within you.

Although Deepak Chopra in his book, *Ageless Body, Timeless Mind,* Bernie Siegel in *Love, Miracles and Medicine,* and other authors do not explicitly identify integrity as the key to the healing processes they are writing about, the body's ability to understand how to restore healthy balance—its integrity—is at the core of the new science of mind/body energy medicine. We have not invented integrity. Rather we are pointing out that this force of nature which is so important in the new healing sciences also has powerful applications in the realm of action.

I can make this abstraction of integrity more concrete through a single image.

In ancient China when the dikes gave way and the floods came and the barbarian hordes poured over the mountains from the west—signifying to the Ruler and his (her) people that the Mandate of Heaven had been lost—only human virtue (*te*) or integrity, the Chinese sages believed, could reverse the challenges of nature. What is the *te*?

THE CHINESE CONCEPT OF "TE"

It is written with a complex character, so beautiful it could be a poem. On the left is the character for "action." Integrity always demands action. On the top right is the character for the number "10," which can also be read "whole" or "balance." Underneath is the character for the number "4," but if this "4" is repositioned and read vertically, the meaning transforms into "eye." Thus there are four "eyes"—the external "eyes" of logic, intelligence and common sense—and then there is the inner eye of direct-knowing or intuition. Four eyes that can see singly as one. Underneath is the character for "heart." Integrity is the state wherein the eye of discovery, logic and intelligence is in balance with the heart in action. See Illustration 1.

Take any person, any situation, and if you examine closely you can tell in an instant the degree of its integrity. Is this person grasping or cunning? Perhaps there is too little heart. Even if by his actions he has become immensely wealthy, there is a flaw (in integrity) that will devour him. Is that a person of great heart and intellect? Perhaps. But can she translate her vision into action? If not there may also be a problem with integrity. Then there are those who

INTEGRITY

Key: ^{1} 彳 = Action

^{2} 十 = Ten, whole balance

3 四 = Four, eye

4 心 = heart

ILLUSTRATION 1

despise logic and navigate through life only by heart. They too are off balance, out of integrity.

Brannan: You seem to be using "integrity" in a very special sense, different from the conventional meaning, which is associated with ethics and morality.

Gresser: Yes, this is true. They are related, of course, but in my view ethics and morality naturally flow from integrity. The truly ethical person is a person whose mind and heart is in balance with action.

Brannan: Once someone understands the algorithm, "integrity," how can this be helpful, at least a source of comfort, when we are frightened or feeling that control over our life is slipping from us?

Gresser: Conceptual understanding is the first step, but it is not enough.

To know your integrity, you must embody it. You don't possess integrity like some physical object or a piece of information. You must live it. This is its great challenge and its lasting worth.

INTEGRITY AS A SKILL

After hundreds of hours of training people all over the world, I have found that integrity is a **skill** which can be learned, developed, and passed on to others. In a way, the practice resembles the inner Chinese martial arts such as tai chi or qi gong. Many of the "moves" by which we cultivate integrity are not seen by others. They take place underneath the surface. Only the results are seen and the changes in our behavior and action.

In the earlier example, it is easy to see how Flanagan outmaneuvered his opponents, his outward moves and tactics. Less obvious are the gradual changes in character that took place only after months of training, the development of his integrity that stabilized the foundation and which enabled him to respond with agility in that difficult situation.

Brannan: How does a player begin to develop the skill of integrity?

Gresser: In my experience, the development of integrity is hastened by the steady cultivation of five core values.

THE FIVE CORE VALUES EARN WHAT YOU WANT

The first is "**earn what you want**." If you would have something you must pay for it—as Emerson says, "line for line, deed for deed, cent for cent." It is in the buyer's interest to pay a just price. It is in the seller's interest to charge it. This is the natural law of compensation. There are no free rides in nature.

Brannan: This requires a bit more explanation. I believe many people feel very good when they purchase or sell something at a real "steal." What's wrong with that? It seems to me they're just getting what the market will bear.

Gresser: We are not trying to introduce some new, even more dour form of Calvinism. If you negotiate effectively, and come away with a bargain from a used car salesman or at a flea market, you've earned what you want. I'm really focusing on the issue of gouging from either the buyer's or the seller's position. What I'm saying is you'll pay a price. Perhaps the price will be in the form of buyer's or seller's remorse, perhaps in a more subtle, indirect way. But there will be repercussions, because things are interconnected. There is an underlying "integrity" in the fabric of human, indeed all natural, interactions and processes. The point is less whether the price is "good" or "bad," "fair" or "unjust." It is hard to find a correct answer to such abstract questions. The critical issue, it seems to me, is are we willing to take the "hit" for our actions? If we are a seller and gouge our clients, are we willing to accept that our clients may leave and go elsewhere? If we are in the market to purchase a house and hoodwink an old lady, are we willing to deal with her executor or her outraged children? If we are willing to take on these things (the "hit"), to pay the price, we will **earn** what we want in the sense I am using it here.

Where and how to take the "hit" is a fundamental question which goes right to the essence of any undertaking. If our purpose is simply to feed our desires we will tend to see the "costs" of our enterprise as detriments. However, if our mission is one of service to others and based on integrity, and if the actions we take truly serve the mission, it is very much in our interest to pay the full price of its attainment. Although this may appear a bit of a paradox at this point, the principle should become clearer when we get into the discussion of mission and purpose in the next chapter.

Brannan: What is the second core value?

Gresser: "**No assumptions, no expectations**." We live in a world that assumes, presumes and consumes everything, and therefore to have no expectations seems an implausible virtue. People are encouraged to have expectations. The law protects them. And yet they entangle us and deplete our energies. In giving them up lies the source of true freedom.

NO ASSUMPTIONS,
NO EXPECTATIONS

Brannan: Yes, but do you really believe for a practical person in business faced with making thousands of quick decisions that this principle is really workable? It seems to me if we make no assumptions we are starting at ground zero every time we begin a negotiation. We always must make decisions based on limited information. Assumptions are useful in filling in the gaps. My view is we must make assumptions and that is okay, so long as we make clear in our planning what items are "assumptions" and what are "facts." Then intelligence is gathered to validate or reject the assumptions.

Gresser: Your point is well taken. What I'm trying to do at this stage, illustrated in the cases to follow, is to show: 1) how we limit our possibilities and thereby impoverish ourselves by not testing our basic assumptions; and 2) how dangerous this habit of making assumptions can be in the practical world of negotiations. Flanagan would have been a dead duck if he hadn't been quick enough to spot his own invalid assumption (intentionally planted by his opponents) that a deal had been reached in Boston.

Brannan: What is the third core value?

Gresser: The next value is "**few needs.**" We must be clear about what we mean by "need." What do we truly need in this life, Tod? Air, water, food, shelter, and a little sleep, but not much more. We don't need success. We don't need strokes—people telling us how wonderful we are. We don't need money, except to provide for our own and our families' welfare and well-being. We don't need fame or security. We don't need approval from the outside world. Therefore we urge people to equip themselves to pass through the chaos of the 1990s by paring down their needs and by taking joy from little triumphs and small, but not insignificant, things.

FEW NEEDS

EMBRACE
THE 'NO'   The fourth core value is "**embrace the 'no.'**"

Brannan: Hey! Hold on. A little too swift. I happen to like my new BMW and I believe most other people enjoy their creature comforts as well. I also don't think you can dismiss so easily the basic human desires—I'd even call them "needs"—for success, praise and love!

Gresser:

Okay, okay! Tod, I'm not urging people to buy a sack cloth and ashes and turn themselves into yogis sitting in caves. Here again the critical issue, it seems to me, is to become **conscious** of how we have been "programmed" and how we program ourselves. Look at the language we use. How many times a day do we sloppily say, "I need to have this" ... or "I need to do that" ... or "I **really** need, because otherwise". . . ? Do we really **need** all these things? All these "needs" are really the voice of the subconscious whispering endlessly to us, "Look, my friend, if you don't feed yourself a little more you'll surely die." That subconscious "need"-voice, Tod, is not your friend. For most, if not all, of these so-called "needs" are delusions! We will not die—that's a fact—if we don't satisfy them.

We've just focused a moment ago on no assumptions/no expectations. How many of these do you think might vanish in an instant if we could let go of our delusory needs? Why, they'd fly right out the window! Letting go of needs is about reaching for freedom.

I realize this practice is not easy. But again, I have observed in the realm of practical action time after time, the negotiator who doesn't need the deal and who can put aside assumptions and expectations is the one who, like Flanagan, will be able to adjust in any contingency and will hold the edge. We must remember also that we are speaking here of skills that cannot be mastered in a day, but take diligence and dedication over weeks and months. Yet these are also skills that in the end will be worth the effort, because they will have lasting value.

The fourth core value, as I say, is **"embrace the 'no.'"**

Since early childhood we have been programmed to believe that we are wrong (bad) when we receive a 'no.' Many children are rebuked by their parents: "Johnny, how many times have I told you, 'No'!" So naturally we feel a need to get to 'yes.' Not achieving an agreement ('yes') is perceived as a failure, a sign of our inadequacy. Yet in my experience a 'no' is a very rich source of wisdom, wonderful conditioning, and often an excellent indication of how and where to move next.

'No' raises another more basic point. In my view every individual has an inalienable **right** to exercise a veto, to say, "I will not submit. I will stand upon my integrity." I am not saying the exercise of this right is costless. You may have to pay a price. But respect for another's right to 'no' and respect for our own right to veto seems to me fundamental.

Therefore we train people not to fear the 'no,' to give the other person space to breathe, to make the tough decisions, which often are the ones that involve a 'no.'

Brannan: The way you present this fourth principle sounds good in theory, but I should think it is very hard to implement in practice, especially if you believe, as most people do, that a 'no' is final. When there is a lot of money and effort at stake, the idea of embracing a 'no' may be hard to swallow.

Gresser: Things do not always turn out as they first seem. The process of negotiation in my experience is rich and unfolding. A 'no' may appear absolute and final at one stage, but then something happens, circumstances change, and the other party discovers a new need we can fulfill and things click when they didn't before. Then too a final 'no' may not be such a bad thing because it almost always opens a new door. I will explain the dynamics of 'no' in action in the discussion of The Five Rings.

Brannan: Four core values so far. What is the last?

Gresser: The fifth and last value has two parts. The first is "**presence is all**." Just as the point of our entire method is integrity, so really there is only one tactic—one tactic that subsumes all others—and it is presence. When we are fully present, we build a foundation, a platform from which springs our creativity, our life force, our ability to discover, to stretch, and to realize our true human potential.

Brannan: Julian, would you say Flanagan was being present or simply "playing dead"? If this is a form of presence, I think you should explain how.

Gresser: Flanagan got a grip. He could have let his needs—his panic—get the better of him, and then he would have become completely unpresent. To put the point more precisely, because he was trained like a fighter pilot, Flanagan knew how in an instant to become present to his panic and to find there his power. It is a very sophisticated concept that I will develop with care and detail later. Panic, as I have said, is one of the ways chaos presents itself. If we can train ourselves to remain present in chaos we will find, as Flanagan did, the path of opportunity.

The corollary of presence is "**Each moment has equal dignity**." Ours is a world where everything, it seems, has unequal dignity, and most people are treated with no dignity.

When we train ourselves to allow each moment its special dignity, then everything has value. When each moment has equal dignity, we live in the eternal present.

II. THE FIVE RINGS

"If we could first know where we are and whither we are tending, we could better judge what to do and how to do it."
— Abraham Lincoln

"Integrity is its own mission and purpose."
— The Artful Navigator

"In his recent concession speech, President de Klerk of South Africa praised his rival, Nelson Mandela, as follows: 'Mr. Mandela has walked a long road and now stands at the top of the hill. A traveler would sit down and admire the view, but a man of destiny knows that beyond this hill lies another and another. The journey is never complete.'"
— The Artful Navigator

II. The Five Rings

Brannan:

Julian, there is a strong sense in your examples and explanation that you believe in the richness of "inner" and "outer" processes and the importance of self-knowledge. But, you know, I'm not sure how many people really think the way you do or will easily accept what you are saying. Just last week I had a curious experience in a plane on my way back from New York that makes this exact point.

I was sitting next to this businessman and we started talking, and he asked me what I did for a living, so I told him a bit about our work together. He was a project manager and said he was constantly involved in negotiations all over the world. When I began to get into the substance of the method he said something that startled me. He said: "Look, I've got a budget. I write the terms. I'm fair, but if the other person is uninterested, that's okay, I just go on to the next one. You see, I'm **in control**! I've been negotiating in this way all over the world for the last 25 years and I have never once needed to know a thing about myself! So why is self-knowledge so important?"

I had some difficulty answering him because it seemed to me the answer was so obvious. Perhaps there are some assumptions about the benefits of self-knowledge that you and I are making that ought to be challenged right at the outset. How would you have responded to that man's question?

Gresser:

Suppose that man loses his precious budget? What will he do? Or what will happen when he grows old or is laid off? Does he assume such things cannot happen? Worse, what if one day he looks in the mirror and discovers a suspicious growth on his neck? He will panic and because he will not know himself he will have no anchor. We live our lives infused with the conceit that we are invincible and immortal, as if our flesh were brass impregnable. But what will happen to this good easy man when, with a little pin, Life bores through his castle walls? Good-bye project manager!

This is what happened to so many stockbrokers at the time of the Great Crash. Not knowing themselves they **identified** with the stockmarket, and when it crashed, they crashed also. They literally jumped out of buildings. They didn't realize they were the players not the pieces.

We must know ourselves first so that we can take back control—adapt and change—at the times when our life begins to shake beneath our feet. And this is perhaps the most important reason a method—a disciplined process—may be of some help.

Brannan: Very well. What is the first step—the first decision— a person must make?

Gresser: To see what he or she truly wants.

Brannan: To see?

Gresser: Yes. Vision drives action. If we cannot see our way through something, it is much harder to do it. Otherwise, we must see our way feelingly. It is a separate art which we can discuss later.

I would like to illustrate how vision enables action by an old story.

VISION DRIVES ACTION

There were once two tribes that made their living by fishing. A great escarpment of mountains divided the two communities, so that no intercourse of any kind was possible.

The dilemma of the first tribe was this.

Although the schools of fish were plentiful, one could never know when the sea gods might withdraw their favors and the fish would swim away. If only there were a way to enter the pools beyond the reef, where it is said the great fish come to play and mate and raise their young. But the elders of the tribe had also said that it was quite impossible to venture that far out, and there had been many attempts and some had perished. And so the village resigned itself.

One day a rumor entered the village that a miracle had occurred among the people beyond the mountains. It seems that someone had come up with an extraordinary invention called a "canoe." By means of this "canoe," people—even the elderly and children—could now journey out beyond the reefs and were feasting on the rich schools of fish.

No knowledge of canoe making of any sort passed across the mountain, only that it was possible to gain access to the pools, and this by means of a "canoe." A few months later, with no other "knowledge" than it was possible, a wood-carver in the second village independently discovered the art of canoe building.

Tod, do you see the point of this story? Simply to acknowledge possibility will change the probabilities. We must allow ourselves the freedom to see the kind of life we want—professionally, personally, physically, spiritually—to brush aside all the beliefs we have become so comfortable in telling ourselves—the beliefs about what is **not** possible. This is the first decision, the first act.

Brannan: And what is the second?

| Gresser: | To prepare a mission and purpose. If you are a pilot and find yourself in an electric storm, how will you feel if your compass fails and your instruments malfunction? Today we are in an electric storm and how many people have the compass intact? The mission and purpose is the pilot's compass. |

| Brannan: | I'm not sure I follow you . . . |

| Gresser:

MISSION AND PURPOSE — THE COMPASS | How many people can tell in an instant in any situation: where they are, where they want to be, or how to get there? Very few. The first, most basic step in knowing how to do these things is to prepare the mission and purpose. The mission and purpose is the reference point. It tells us instantly where we have come from, where we are heading, when we fall off, and how to get ourselves back on course. |

| Brannan: | How does one go about preparing a mission? |

| Gresser: | The first decision, the first step I recommend is for the listener to set aside some afternoon or evening, a few hours, and in this space of time to reflect deeply on the following two questions, in each of the four quadrants in life: professional, personal, physical, spiritual. |

- **What is it I really want?**

This "really" is the key, because, as I have suggested and will explain in more detail later, it is essential at this stage to stretch, to brush aside all the baggage about what is **not** possible. We want them to get in touch with what truly matters.

And the second question is:

- **How can I best earn what I want with the gifts I**

now have (i.e., my resources, my contacts, my station in life, and so forth)?

We **earn** what we want by connecting our gifts to the concerns of others. In this sense, the mission is a **path of service**, for nothing in this life comes free except the air.

After one has reflected upon these two questions I ask my students to compose a single statement of mission. It does not have to be lengthy. The key is to capture in a few powerful strokes what they want, and how by using their gifts and resources, they propose to get there.

Brannan: Can you give some examples?

Gresser: All right. Here is a **physical** mission statement: "To build health and vitality so that I can live an abundant and vibrant life that will permit me to realize my true gifts and make whatever contribution I am here to make." Note even here the element of service. We seek vitality, not for ourselves alone, but also because it helps us realize why we are here.

People may have widely different objectives in their physical life and the means of achieving these missions may also differ greatly. The means are incorporated within the mission statement. A person might write: "I will accomplish this mission through vigorous exercise in my favorite sports of tennis, golf, and windsurfing, and by long hikes in the mountains, where I return to the wellspring of my true nature."

Brannan: What about a professional mission, for example, the mission of our own enterprise, Lōgōs Networks Corporation.

Gresser: Our mission is clear. It states in part: "To put in the hands of dedicated persons a proven means by which to build integrity, which will enhance their ability to discover, to take greater delight in their work and their pastimes, and to navigate effectively through the chaos of the 1990s and whatever may come after."

The statement of means would then identify those areas of our experience and expertise that will help us accomplish this mission, for example, my knowledge and experience in Japan and other parts of Asia, your many years in building computer systems and networks that are easy to operate and fun to use.

Brannan: How does this exercise in mission building relate to integrity?

Gresser: A good question. Most people live fragmented and scattered lives; for example, their professional life is divorced from their personal life. They are so driven they scarcely have time to re-create themselves physically or spiritually. The process of building a life mission and with it a sense of life purpose will itself begin to restore coherence, wholeness, a sense of connection and vitality, which is how we define integrity.

AM I HERE BY INTEGRITY?   Whenever we are lost or confused, there is only one question that need be asked: "How does this next decision or action reinforce my overall mission?" If the next decision fails to do this, or if the situation you are in will undermine your mission, instantly you know you must adjust. On the other hand, if your next decision or action advances your mission, you can know with certainty you are on the right track. You will know you are here by integrity.

Brannan: Could you elaborate a bit on the concept of coherence of missions?

Gresser: This is an important point. I have found it useful to think of missions as building both "horizontal" and "vertical" coherence. For example, few people recognize any direct relationship between their physical exercise and their professional work. But when the underlying objective is to cultivate integrity, then the interplay of these two life quadrants becomes clear (horizontal coherence).

COHERENCE OF MISSIONS

Do you remember, Tod, when I asked you what was one of the great challenges in your life as a tennis player?

Brannan: I remember well.

Gresser: And you reported, "To beat my chief opponent. I always lose to X. What I really want is to win."

Brannan: Yes, that's what I said.

Gresser: And what then happened?

Brannan: You suggested I was so focused on the result, on winning, that I was losing focus on the present. So I resolved to forget about winning altogether, and just to concentrate on the ball, and my game has improved.

Gresser: That's it. Just concentrate on the ball! By improving your tennis skills—learning to stay present or to maintain focus, for example—you improve your negotiation skills, because they are essentially the same skill set. Thus perfecting your tennis game can strongly advance your professional mission! The process of developing integrity is what encourages these "overlaps" in our professional, personal, physical and spiritual lives, and we begin to discover interconnections among the parts we never thought possible before.

By "vertical" coherence, I refer to the hierarchy of missions. You and I have overall professional missions in which our work with Logos Networks Corporation (LNC) is a part; and under LNC we may have several main projects, each of which will have its own subordinate mission. And within each of these projects we may have hundreds of matters or cases, again each containing its own ancillary mission.

THE HIERARCHY OF MISSIONS

Most people are unaware of the interplay of these various activities. No one stops to ask, how does this matter advance my "higher" project mission, or how does this project really enhance my overall professional mission?

By taking the time to ask such questions—and there always is the time if we truly want to make the time—by learning to adjust, align, and when necessary, to stretch, we build stability and solidity in our life, which leads to a deeper sense of meaning, vitality and promise.

Brannan:

A mission implies an allocation of resources.

Gresser:

Yes, that is true. It is one thing to know what we want, and where to aim, i.e., the mission, quite another to make a commitment—and the commitment is key—to allocate our scarce resources in that direction. The question is what are our available resources? This brings me to the subject of the budget.

BUDGET = TIME X EFFORT X FINANCIAL RESERVES X CREATIVE VITALITY

There are four elements in what we call "budget." They are time, to which we assign a value of "1"; effort with a value of "2"; financial reserves with a value of "3"; and creative emotion or vitality with a value of "4." By "value," I refer to the relative importance in a negotiation of each of these four elements. In other words, creative emotion or vitality is four times as valuable as time; financial reserves are worth three times time; and effort twice as much.

These ratios are not precise nor based on extensive academic research. Rather they derive from the personal experience of thousands of hours of negotiations.

At the outset, we urge people when beginning to work with us to make a **conscious** allocation of these critical elements of budget in the four quadrants of their life.

We refer to these elements in the aggregate as "integrity budget units" (IBUs) because, as we will see, integrity can be enhanced or disturbed by how wisely we expend these resources. The first task is to come up with an overall budget in terms of IBUs covering in a 24-hour day how we propose to expend these four critical elements in our professional, personal, physical and spiritual lives.

People's allocations differ greatly and no one formula is correct. One person may allocate IBUs in his life equally, i.e., 25% professional, 25% physical, 25% personal, 25% spiritual. Another person might allocate 50% to her professional matters and subdivide the remainder equally. Others may shift allocations over time. In my case, for example, launching our enterprise has consumed enormous amounts of IBUs and there has been a price—a great price—I and my family (and I'm sure yours also) have had to pay. There has also been a great cost charged against all the things I enjoy and like to do in other quadrants of my life. Soon I will make some adjustments. Such allocations and sacrifices are largely personal and there is no one correct solution. The mission statements and your own integrity are your best guides. The essential point—which cannot be emphasized enough—is to become **conscious**, for when we become aware of how we are expending our precious reserves, what we will sacrifice and for what purpose, we can begin to make intelligent decisions, to adjust, and to apply these resources to their best possible uses.

Brannan: You know, Julian, it occurs to me that we have become so comfortable with setting IBUs it almost seems second nature. But this practice may seem quite alien, especially to people who are not involved as we are in business.

Gresser: Your comment raises an important point for both business and non-business persons. For some people engaged in business who like measuring things, the value of tracking IBUs may be immediately obvious. But others may dismiss the technique on the grounds that it is not really possible to aggregate in any meaningful way the different elements of budget, i.e., time, effort, financial reserves and creative vitality. Possibly non-business persons will wave their hands in dismay, believing the technique to be simply too remote from the way they think.

And yet, when we look a bit more deeply into the practices of many artists and other creative people, I believe you will find, as I have, that they do in fact have an accounting system—perhaps not as formal as ours—but nonetheless a systematic way to husband their time and creative energies. For example, I know many writers and almost all of them have a special time of day in which they write, and they are very disciplined about guarding this window of creativity from intruders, be they children, spouses, friends or clients. It is very clear to them that their creativity is not a "free good" and that unless they develop some intelligent way to conserve their precious resource, they will squander it.

For me, the bottom line for both business and non-business readers is this: We make no claim to scientific precision. We have developed an accounting procedure that we have found to be easy to use and helpful in achieving the objectives of the method. Many persons involved in business and outside of business will, I believe, also find this technique helpful. Some persons may simply not find it their cup of tea. The key point, however, is that our readers develop for themselves some practical way to account for expenditures of their scarce resources of time, effort, financial reserves and creativity, for to do otherwise is unconsciously to assign a value—indeed a value probably inconsistent with their true feelings—and that value will be zero.

Brannan: Let us return to the main concourse and review where we are. We have moved from the theory of integrity and the five core values to the beginning of the discussion of the "method." You suggested that the first step is to get in touch with what we truly want and then to build a mission in the four quadrants of life. At that point a person is in a position to begin to decide how he or she wishes to divide up the available time, effort, financial reserves, and creative vitality that comprise the "life pie."

Suppose someone is willing to invest the time you say is required to do this—and I believe you noted that it would take only a few hours—how can he or she immediately begin to enter the fray?

Gresser: I call our method "The Five Rings." It provides a way to analyze the structure and flow of our decisions and those of others, and to negotiate effectively in any situation. Each ring presents an opportunity to develop integrity in a focused way through the cultivation of the five core values.

Brannan: Before you explain The Five Rings, Julian, it is important to define "negotiation," because you appear to be using the term in a very special and uncustomary way.

Gresser: Thank you for making this point. In the method I adopt the third definition of negotiation in Webster's New International Dictionary, "To move forward successfully, to get across or through an obstacle," as "to negotiate a river or to negotiate the mountains." "Negotiation" is the process of moving any cause forward. To give you a sense of how important this definition can be, when do you suppose, Tod, Flanagan's negotiation with his Japanese colleagues ended?

Brannan: I would imagine when they reached a final agreement to invest in the technology joint venture.

Gresser: That is what most people in business might suppose. The negotiations end when we reach agreement, when we obtain a 'yes.' Actually, that is when Flanagan's real negotiation was just beginning. "Real" in the sense that he was at great risk if he believed the play had ended, at exactly the time his opponents were marshalling their forces for the next attack. Because Flanagan was "trainable" he caught on quickly to the danger he was in. He did not assume a negotiation was over simply because an agreement had been reached. In playing the "game" of integrity the negotiation with ourself and others also never ends. The method, The Five Rings, is a means to keep us alert.

THE FIVE RINGS   In an instant, it allows you to determine:

- Where you are
- Where you want to be
- How to get there
- How to adjust to change
- How to correct error
- What is the best next move

(See Illustration 2.)

Brannan: What is the first ring?

Gresser: The first ring is called, "Know Yourself." Its purpose is to help you set your course and to build a plan of action. Ring 1 contains several basic moves. They are:

RING 1 -
KNOW YOURSELF
- Get clear about what you really want in any negotiation or encounter.
- Build a mission or path of action.
- Set your budget in terms of IBUs.
- Devise a simple plan.
- Initiate the first action.

The mission, the budget, the plan, and the initiating action are all specific to the engagement.

There is something now you should notice about each of the "moves" in Ring 1, and it holds true of the entire method. I want you to focus on this question: What can we manage?

Brannan: Time and money . . . I'm not sure. Many people believe they are "managing" when in fact they are completely out of control.

Gresser: Precisely. Can we manage numerical results?

Brannan: Hardly.

Gresser: I agree. We can never manage numerical results, and

THE FIVE RINGS

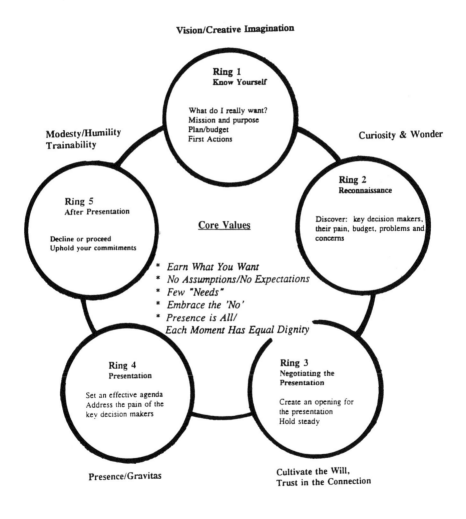

Vision/Creative Imagination

Ring 1
Know Yourself

What do I really want?
Mission and purpose
Plan/budget
First Actions

Modesty/Humility
Trainability

Curiosity & Wonder

Ring 5
After Presentation

Decline or proceed
Uphold your commitments

Core Values

Ring 2
Reconnaissance

Discover: key decision makers,
their pain, budget, problems and
concerns

* *Earn What You Want*
* *No Assumptions/No Expectations*
* *Few "Needs"*
* *Embrace the 'No'*
* *Presence is All/*
Each Moment Has Equal Dignity

Ring 4
Presentation

Set an effective agenda
Address the pain of the
key decision makers

Ring 3
Negotiating the
Presentation

Create an opening for
the presentation
Hold steady

Presence/Gravitas

Cultivate the Will,
Trust in the Connection

ILLUSTRATION 2

yet how many businesses distribute benefits or impose penalties or make their fundamental policy decisions based on numerical results? The best way to put an athlete, an employee, or a sales person in a slump is to tell them they must hit ten home runs, bill X thousands of dollars, or sell Y units by the end of such-and-such a quarter. Numerical results can be a useful guideline, but determining success and failure by a single numerical index simply invites frantic and unproductive performance.

Next. Can we manage other people's actions and behavior?

Brannan: I doubt it.

Gresser: Throughout history all sorts of people, particularly despots, have tried and always they have failed. A wonderful book on this subject is Victor Frankl's *Man's Search for Meaning*, which recounts how he survived the Nazi death camps at Auschwitz. In an especially poignant passage he describes how, under the most egregious conditions, the prisoners struggled to retain their last power to choose—to choose to see and appreciate beauty.

From the window of a boxcar being transported to another work detail he writes:

> "If someone had seen our faces on the journey from Auschwitz to a Bavarian camp as we beheld the mountains of Salzburg with their summits glowing in the sunset, through the little barred windows of the prison carriage, he would never have believed that those were the faces of men who had given up all hope of life and liberty. Despite that factor—or maybe because of it—we were carried away by

nature's beauty, which we had missed for so long."

If even the Nazis could not completely stamp out in the minds of their prisoners the instinct toward choice, why do we presume we can manage how other people will think, believe or act?

One last point, Tod. Can we manage time?

Brannan: I believe so. There are many time management courses around . . .

Gresser: I know about the courses. But can we ever manage the flow of time? No. Time flows on and on and we fools of nature like small craft are carried away on the great current no matter how we tell ourselves otherwise.

Here is the critical point. In negotiations we will get ourselves in terrible difficulty if we allow ourselves to believe we can ever manage or control numerical results, other people's actions or the flow of time. Because we cannot manage these things, in our frustration and despair we will fall into need, lose hope, and our integrity will be impaired. For this reason the moves in Ring 1 and throughout The Five Rings focus us on our own actions and behavior over which we have some large measure of control. By asserting ourselves here we gain some incremental margin of influence over the uncertain and destabilizing forces of life.

Brannan: On this same theme of reclaiming an edge, what about situations where someone is really out at sea? Are there any default moves?

Gresser: Ring 1, as all the other rings, has its "default" moves, so that if at any moment you cannot see what to do, the method will help you. Suppose a player jumps over the first few steps right into the thick of action, for example, makes a phone call or has a meeting without a clue as to what she really wants and without a mission. Then suppose this player begins to observe that things are not going quite as well as she hoped, that there is some kind of "problem." The method provides an instant "diagnosis": "No mission, I am not clear about what I want." The default move is equally explicit: Regroup, clarify, prepare a simple mission. If you do these things with full awareness and presence, you will instantly feel your powers collecting and your integrity building.

The five core values apply to each ring and to every part of it. Each ring provides a practical context and an opportunity to practice.

Each ring also offers a unique opportunity to develop special powers. For example, Ring 1 presents an opportunity to develop vision and to harness the power of creative imagination to intentionality.

Brannan: You have mentioned the story of the fishing villages and how by dropping the "delusion" of impossibility the second village began to discover a solution to its dilemma. How might the same principle apply in business?

Gresser: I will tell you. In the mid-1980s when I was working in Japan I conceived the idea of taking foreign companies public on the Tokyo Over-The-Counter Market. I wrote a letter to a friend at Arthur Andersen setting out how my strategy might be practically accomplished. I didn't hear anything for six months. One day I received a phone call from my friend saying he had found a candidate. The candidate was Getz Brothers, a San Francisco-based trading company that had established a respectable market share in Japan importing pacemakers, heart valves, catheters, and other cardiovascular products. Getz had $8 million in net income based upon approximately $70 million in general revenues.

No one was interested in the project. Getz was virtually unknown outside its industry. It had no products of its own and its business was highly vulnerable because it was based on short-term distribution contracts of other companies' products. The leading American underwriters, Goldman Sachs and Morgan Stanley, would not even return our phone calls after the first hour. (By now we were a team of two, the acting president and I.) The Japanese government immediately told us that our plan was not possible. We were not public in any other market and there was a "rule" stipulating that no foreign company could go public on the Tokyo Over-The-Counter market unless it was publicly registered in another country. We were operating through a branch and there was another rule, we were told, prohibiting branches from going public.

In short, everything was impossible!

But we could see possibility through other people's impossibility and so we began. We did some research and found that Japanese companies could in fact go public under the U.S. NASDAQ rules. The restriction on non-public companies appeared to violate the principle of reciprocity in liberalizing the Japanese capital markets which the Japanese government had only months before recognized. We negotiated and obtained a concession on this point. Next we set up a wholly-owned subsidiary and transferred the assets of Getz's branch into this new company. This solved the objection relating to the branch. In the subsequent months we negotiated hard on a hundred other objections.

It is a long story with many curves and reverses. In the end we prevailed. Three years later Getz went public with a capitalized market value of $450 million. Two years later its value had climbed to over $1 billion, and several years after that the owners sold the company for $1.2 billion—and this despite the fact that the Japanese economic bubble had burst and many foreign and Japanese companies were suffering drastic deteriorations in their stock values.

We paid little heed to what people told us was "impossible," we knew what we wanted, we had a clear mission and negotiated with determination based on integrity.

Brannan: Tell us something about Ring 2.

Gresser: Ring 2 is called "Reconnaissance." Its purpose is to identify the "decision makers" who can make what we want happen. We are after answers to these essential questions:

RING 2
RECONNAISSANCE

- What is their pain?
- What is their available budget (in the sense we have already discussed)?
- What problems, concerns or reservations do they have that might impede taking effective action?

Brannan: It is important that you elaborate on the concept of "pain" because, really, it seems fundamental to the entire method.

Gresser: Yes, that's true. Most of the world's great spiritual traditions take suffering as their point of departure. Pain is also the crucible of discovery. In *Agamemnon*, Aeschylus writes in the voice of the Chorus, "He leads us on the way of wisdom's everlasting law that truth is only learned by suffering it."

pain

By "pain," we refer not only to calamity. A joy that is unrealized or frustrated can also be painful because there is a gap between our hopes, aspirations, and present reality. This gap can be very painful. In Ring 2 we seek to understand the pain of others, and then to decide what is the best way to help them see their pain. If they fail to see their pain—and many people try to bury unpleasant things or to escape from them—they will not be able to discover the path that will lead them out of pain. That is our task—our basic mission—to link what we want to the pain of those who are in a position to make what we want happen, to help them see their pain, and then to help them discover the path to take it away.

You know, Tod, behind this discussion of pain there are also some important insights into the behavioral dynamics of decision making. Shall I outline these?

Brannan:

Yes, please do.

Gresser:

How would you answer this question: Are decisions made rationally or emotionally, and in what proportion?

Brannan:

I'm not sure. I suppose it depends.

Gresser:

EMOTIONS AND DECISION MAKING

I have observed that decisions are almost invariably made emotionally, 100%, and rationalized thereafter. The decision makers will first reach an emotional decision ('yes' or 'no') to embrace our cause, and later they will rationalize it. And the principal source of this emotion is pain. If you can understand the emotional source, you will understand the direction in which that person will move, and you will be better able to guide them to an effective decision.

Brannan:

This emphasis upon the emotional element in decision making appears quite at odds with how many people, particularly thinking professionals, view what they are doing.

Gresser: Take Supreme Court Justice Steven Breyer, for example. During the Senate Judiciary Committee Hearings Senator Paul Simon asked Justice Breyer, "Will there be someone who will speak for those who are least fortunate in our society?" And Justice Breyer answered, "I hope so," noting, however, that most of his written opinions expressed what is in his head rather than in his heart. He continued, "Judge Wisdom (the esteemed Court of Appeals Judge John Minor Wisdom) gave me some good advice. He said if you feel you want to write a purple passage because you feel so strongly, write it and don't use it, because people want your result and are not necessarily interested in your feelings . . . what I'll try to do is set out the facts as dispassionately as possible, for the facts will speak for themselves, and that can have an impact, too. That's how I've approached it."

In my experience there is a continuing dialogue between emotions and the intellect, but the emotions drive the chariot and the intellect holds on as best it can to the reins.

Brannan: What else happens in Ring 2?

Gresser: In Ring 2 we must stay close to the earth, testing our principal assumptions, and continuously reminding
CURIOSITY   ourselves, "What is this? . . . let me explore a bit more
AND WONDER   . . . perhaps I really don't know." In Ring 2 all the senses are engaged, especially the eyes which are curious and seeking and full of wonder.

Brannan: To unveil the key decision makers, to understand their pain, to assess their budget, and to explore their problems and reservations may be easy in some circumstances but very hard in others.

Gresser: True enough. There are many barriers that frustrate reconnaissance, particularly so in transacting business in foreign countries. Take Japan, for example. The Japanese are past masters in deploying blockers, agents, and scouts. The key decision makers, referred to poetically as "the dragon in the clouds" (kumo no ryū) or "the black curtain" (kuromaku), are often never seen. At the same time the Japanese government's intelligence network is superb. The purpose of an agent or scout is to plant or draw out information, usually with the adversary utterly unaware of what is happening.

Brannan: Can you give an example?

Gresser: Yes. During the past 25 years in which I have studied the Japanese system of negotiation, I have come upon a hidden code consisting of over a hundred basic moves and tactics, some of which are so sophisticated and culturally embedded that they are hidden even from the Japanese themselves. The subject of the code is really a separate and fascinating discussion. But here is a case that captures the flavor.

Some years ago a West Coast architectural firm had encountered difficulty in obtaining payment for the services it had rendered a Japanese designer. After months of excuses and delay the president approached me and asked for my help. I prepared a "pain" letter which contained this key clause. "After all the years it has taken to develop a reputation in Japan as a lead designer—particularly all the hurdles and frustrations you have had to surmount, as a professional woman in Japanese society, why would you want to have your reputation tarnished and become known as someone who walks away from her commitments?"

The letter containing this sentence was approved and, I assumed, duly sent out.

Weeks passed. I did not hear from the president. About two months later I got a call from him asking me to attend a strategy meeting. The bill remained unpaid.

During the meeting the actual letter which had been sent to the designer was being passed around the table. I glanced at it casually. To my surprise the key section, "**particularly all the hurdles and frustrations you have had to surmount, as a professional woman in Japanese society,**" had been deleted! The sentence was crucial because it focused the spotlight clearly on the price she had paid to reach her level of professional accomplishment in Japan and the price she must now pay in losing her good name.

"What's going on?" I asked the president. "What happened to the sentence we worked on together, the one pointing out the risks to her reputation as a professional woman in Japan?"

"Sachiko didn't think it was a good idea," the president told me definitively.

"Who's Sachiko?" I asked, puzzled.

"Oh, Sachiko is our new cultural coordinator. She said that your sentence was very offensive, and that under no circumstances must we ever offend if we want to do business in Japan."

Sachiko was a recent 23-year-old graduate student in psychology. She was sincere, dedicated, and generally wanted to be of service to the architectural firm. She was also an unwitting spy. Her actions were culturally programmed, hard wired. She was completely unaware of the damage she was causing.

The president corrected the error, sent out a second letter, and was back in the game in a few weeks.

Several months later, in response to increasing pressure, the designer came to San Francisco and a satisfactory accommodation was worked out. But the most basic first step was getting around the agent/scout and dealing with the designer directly.

Brannan: What about default moves in Ring 2?

Gresser: If in the midst of reconnaissance, a player starts to feel out of control, as with Ring 1, there are always safe harbors.

Negotiation is rarely about telling and almost always about asking and discovery. If you have not obtained even initial answers to the basic questions in Ring 2, you are well advised to default to Ring 1, as you may have more work to do on your intention, your mission or plan of action.

If you are still dissatisfied with the answers you have received, you may wish to refine your questions in the next round, and to nurture the other players' discovery process more carefully.

It is very important not to negotiate a presentation (Ring 3) until you are reasonably certain to whom you should present (i.e., the key decision makers). If you are still unclear, you have more work to do in Ring 2.

The core values of **earning what you want,** no assumptions, no expectations, **embrace the 'no,' presence**, and **each moment has equal dignity**, all directly apply in Ring 2. They are always the safest harbors.

Brannan: What is Ring 3 about?

Gresser: In formal terms, the purpose of Ring 3 is to position yourself optimally for your presentation. To do this you must:

1. Help the key decision makers begin vividly to see their pain. It is an act of compassion.

2. Navigate effectively, like Magellan, around all the external obstacles, the blockers, spies, agents and scouts, and also through the internal impediments we ourselves set up to obstruct our own progress.

In Ring 3 you must become even clearer about who is really making the decisions, what is their pain, their budget, and any problems or concerns that will impede their reaching an effective decision.

There will be tests. Your challenge is to hold steady, to manage your resources wisely, and to keep advancing the mission.

One of the key tests in Ring 3 is what I call "no dumping, no spilling." "No dumping" refers to letting your emotions bleed out. "No spilling" refers to the spilling of information, in both cases, to blockers, agents, spies, false decision makers, or to people who may not have your good interests at heart. To spill or dump under circumstances where you have not laid a proper foundation for presenting this information is almost always risky.

No one is immune. Spilling happens to ordinary persons and to presidents. For example, some years ago President George Bush visited Japan, ostensibly to urge the Japanese to open their domestic automobile market. I don't know whom he thought he was negotiating with, but at a formal State dinner he spilled his case (literally) all over Prime Minister Miyazawa who most certainly wasn't the real decision maker. With even a modicum of preparatory work in Ring 2, the President's mission to Japan might have been far more successful. A Japanese friend who observed this spectacle remarked to me at the time in disgust, "President Bush is a dragon without clouds," by which he meant a decision maker who makes himself available and doesn't have the sense to remain in the shadows.

Ring 3 involves not only tactical maneuvers around blockers, scouts and agents, it also provides a wonderful opportunity to develop character. Ring 3 is the space in which often the darkness envelops us—for example, we are betrayed, we lose hope, we get nowhere; doubts, fears and obsessions all rise to the surface and whisper to us, "Give up, you cannot do this, why even try?" I call these the Voices of the Trolls, who seek to shipwreck us on the rocks of our emotions, insecurity and vanity.

Brannan: What can be done?

Gresser: We must remain steady—to see the darkness as an opening and a challenge to our Will to carry on, no matter what the consequences and in spite of all reverses.

Do you remember Churchill's famous speech which aroused the fighting spirit of England during one of the darkest and most perilous periods of World War II?

> "We shall not flag or fail. We shall go on to the end. We shall fight in France, we shall fight on the seas and oceans, we shall fight with growing confidence and growing strength in the air, we shall defend our island, whatever the cost may be. We shall fight on the beaches, we shall fight on the

landing grounds, we shall fight in the fields and in the streets, we shall fight in the hills; we shall never surrender."

His was a giant Will.

Gresser: You know, Tod, every man and woman, and even small children, can cultivate this spirit of fearlessness, to move through the darkest times into the light. I have a client, a Swedish builder of prefab houses, who has been inveigled by five companies belonging to one of the giant Japanese conglomerates. With the encouragement of the Swedish and Japanese governments, he entered into a joint venture partnership to build and sell Swedish houses throughout Japan, including the construction of an entire Swedish village in Hokkaido. He dedicated his factory to supply the venture, he hired architects and designers, and worked for over four years without pay to prepare a unique system of construction. But as soon as his partners obtained his know-how, they defaulted on the deal, violated his copyrights, refused to purchase materials and parts from his factory, which caused him great financial hardship, and then seized the factory when it went into bankruptcy.

When we met three years ago, he was despairing. The first thing we did was to build a mission of service. I told him, "If you focus only upon your personal grievances, your sense of outrage, few people will rally to your cause. You must link your grievances to the concerns of others. Therein lies your power."

And that is what he did. He resolved to spend his time, his honor and his money in helping other Swedish business people and the Swedish government (if it would listen) to learn from his personal misfortune and to become more adept in their Japanese negotiations.

He has spent the last few years mostly in Ring 3. It has been a productive time, and he has rebuilt his damaged integrity. He has learned to take joy from little victories and to profit from his many errors, frustrations and defeats. And still he carries on with humor, dignity and balance, steadfastly working on his mission to obtain fair compensation and to help other Swedes deal more vigilantly with Japanese companies and the Japanese government.

He has made much progress. Gradually many Swedes are waking up to the real game that is being played by the Japanese Embassy, the Japanese government and by the big Japanese companies in Sweden. As of this writing, he has secured two court decisions confirming that his company is the rightful owner of the copyrights, and that his adversaries have infringed, and continue to infringe, these copyrights. A member of the Swedish royal family has written to the Japanese Vice Foreign Minister requesting that the dispute be amicably resolved. The Swedish police have become involved. A member of the Japanese Diet (Parliament) has questioned officials of the Japanese Ministry of Construction and has learned that, despite the recent earthquakes in Kobe, Osaka and Sakhalin Island, in which over 7,000 people have died, the Japanese Ministry of Construction never bothered to test houses that were imported by the conglomerate from a rival supplier after three of the companies repudiated their agreement with my client.

We have discovered that 600 families, including many children, are now living in these houses which have not been tested for earthquakes, and no one has cared to warn them.

The battle continues and I believe in the end the Swedish builder will win—if "winning" means he will receive fair compensation. But in another sense he has already won. He has moved far along toward accomplishing his public mission and his experience has deepened him greatly. He is a much wiser and, for this, a richer man.

Brannan: What are the default moves in Ring 3?

Gresser: The most basic rule of Ring 3 is: be careful about spilling information or dumping emotions prematurely to non-decision makers. We are "programmed" to spill, and therefore much of this behavior may be unconscious. However, if you spill prematurely, you may find that you are falling into "need" and your later presentation may be less effective.

Brannan: How are we programmed to spill?

Gresser: In our universities, for example, most professors lecture rather than listen or really seek to learn from their students. The students are rewarded more on what they write or publish than by how much they truly understand and can embody their understanding in action.

Brannan: What can you do if you have spilled prematurely by making a presentation to a non-decision maker, for example, to a blocker?

Gresser: You should seriously consider withdrawing the presentation, as I will explain in a moment, and returning to the basic task of helping the key decision makers see their pain more clearly. Moreover, if you still do not have a good understanding of the key questions, i.e., who makes the decisions, by what process, what is their pain, what is their negotiating budget, or what are their problems or reservations (i.e., their agenda), you have a clear signal that you should not proceed to Ring 4, and that substantial work remains in Rings 2 and 3.

Brannan: What are the elements of Ring 4?

Gresser: Ring 4, Presentation, creates an opening. Our task is
                simply to attend. To remain present and steady in
RING 4   action—when we fall or when we ascend—is perhaps
PRESENTATION the critical survival skill of this or any other age. So
                if you stumble—lose your sense of connectedness,
                presence, or *gravitas*—take note of the error. You may
                learn something valuable in Ring 4 that will serve you
                well in any situation.

                Ring 4 has a few useful rules that can be summarized
                in five questions.

                First, **what** is the decision you seek? The more pre-
                cisely you can define this decision, the more on
                point will be your presentation.

                Second, **to** whom should you present? The basic rule
                is to focus on **who** is in a position to make the **deci-
                sion** you want. We are not interested in the theoret-
                ical decision makers. For example, do not assume that
                the key person is necessarily the head of a division.
                The real decision maker may be the president or the
                chief executive officer. But the top dog may not be
                the key person. Often underlings run the show. It
                takes discipline and patience to ferret out who are
                the real decision makers.

                The third question is **when** to present? The presen-
                tation step in Ring 4 demands that we contain our-
                selves, in other words, to "hold" integrity. Before we
                present our case, our proposal, our product or ser-
                vice, we must determine the other person's pain and
                budget. As I indicated earlier, the art of negotiation
                is to help others come to terms with their deepest joys
                and sorrows, i.e., the pain, and then to help them dis-
                cover the path to take it away. If we do not know the

pain, or if the decision makers cannot see their pain, what use will be our presentation?

The same principle holds true of budget. Why present to someone who does not possess a budget, or who will not make available time and effort, financial reserves, or creativity? Enterprises without an adequate budget are usually ill-starred.

Brannan: What about the agenda for a presentation?

Gresser: I'm coming to that. Establishing a valid agenda is another precondition of an effective presentation. As with budget, you will run into trouble if you present your case prematurely without first establishing a context or a foundation. I call the foundation, the "agenda."

A valid agenda has five elements. They are:

1.   "Real" or objective problems.

2.   The other party's issues, reservations or concerns which may erupt into serious difficulties or problems at a later date.

3.   Our concerns and reservations.

4.   What we want.

5.   What happens next.

We must endeavor to address all these issues **before presenting**, because otherwise they can rise up and haunt us. Again, this tendency is particularly vexing in transacting business in countries like Japan, where reticence is highly valued. Many American negotiators conclude what they believe to be a final agreement, hold a victory celebration, and then are flabbergasted when the Japanese negotiators raise new concerns or objections. Such cases vividly point out the clash of cultures at the "agenda" step—the need of Americans to reach for clarity and certainty, the appreciation of the Japanese, the Chinese and other East Asian societies, of uncertainty and ambiguity.

Brannan: What is the fourth question?

Gresser: **Where**—the issue of venue. Here we must balance the desirability of making the decision as easy as possible for the other party against the cost to us of our doing so (see budget). Should we drive to their office or place of business? Again the best way to answer such questions is to determine first how significant this person's decision is to our mission. You must ask yourself, will the potential benefits of this decision exceed their actual costs to me in time, effort, financial reserves, and creative vitality?

Brannan: What is the last question?

Gresser: **How**. After we determine to whom and when to present, the final critical question is: **how**? As I have said, the key is full presence. We take the pain of our opponents and their concerns, one by one, in the order of their importance to **them**, and we help them see how each of these issues can be effectively addressed. We do so simply and clearly, without wobbling, exaggeration or adornment. Remember, the goal is to stir their emotions and to help them see—by their hearts and stomachs—the possibility of hope for a solution.

The principles of formal presentation are straightforward. When we attend fully—embodying the five core values—we will provide just enough information and in the time available. Many people incorrectly believe that they must cover "everything." But "everything" is a bottomless pit. Your presentation will exactly fit the requirements of the setting if you will let your integrity be your guide. People judge not only by contents of the message. The superior person will look underneath the data for the intangible, subtle clues and signals in which you reveal who you really are.

Brannan: Have you covered all the elements?

Gresser: There is one more thing.

Brannan: What is that?

Gresser: After you present in the manner I have described, you must allow the other party space to reject your presentation. You must acknowledge their right to say 'no.'

Brannan: It will be hard for many people to digest this.

Gresser: I agree. But the principle fits squarely with the core values. Most people associate a 'no' with failure, a loss, a mistake, or simply with being wrong. In point of fact a 'no' is none of these. It is simply a decision, like any other decision.

'NO'   Do you understand why a 'no' can place an untrained person in a predicament, for example, when he/she rejects a valid proposal because of price or some other condition? The rejecting party is in pain, and we, the presenter, hold the solution. If we graciously acknowledge the 'no,' I have found bonding may actually take place, particularly if the pain is unresolved. I have seen many cases where 'no' is first given and graciously received, and then weeks pass and more resources are invested in finding a solution to the original problem, and then in the end the 'no'-giver relents and in exasperation pays a far higher price for the original services that were offered.

A 'no' can be of great benefit to us in other ways. A 'no' helps us rationalize the uses of our own scarce resources. A 'no' says, "invest here, not there." Also a 'no' is wonderful conditioning—a hit—like a cold bracing shower. In time, as the pain of receiving a 'no' recedes, so will our need, and the more we allow 'nos' to strip away illusory needs and allow us to live simply, the freer we become. It is also axiomatic that those who can receive a 'no' in good humor are also better able to exercise the veto, which is a critical skill of leadership.

Brannan: If one runs into trouble in Ring 4, what are some of the default moves?

Gresser: The most common difficulty involves multiple decision makers. In most large organizations it is commonplace for many people to be involved in an important decision. In such cases you must negotiate hard to make your own presentation, to stand or to fall upon your own sword. It can be a serious error to allow another party, who is untrained or may have a different agenda or be under different pressures, to plead your case. Even if that person is well-disposed toward you, he (or she) may unwittingly sabotage your presentation.

In these situations an intelligent course is to present to **all** the key decision makers simultaneously. If this is not feasible, you must negotiate an agreement from one of the key players that, if your presentation is convincing, he/she will facilitate a meeting with all the others. In this negotiation you must help that person see the potential for embarrassment, of attempting to sell you or your product, service or cause, with inadequate information. If the party remains adamant, the default move may be to return to Ring 3, lay a new foundation and devise a new strategy for a later presentation.

If your presentation becomes confused and you sense you are losing your bearings, just relax, be friendly, and return to the other party's dreams, concerns and frustrations.

If you sense your presentation is premature or incomplete, you may decide to table or even to withdraw it. You might apologize: "You know, I have more work to do in understanding how I can be of real service to you. With what you have told us, I would like to revise our proposal and see if it will not address even more clearly the issues you are struggling with."

If your integrity tells you that you are pressing too hard and the other side begins to move away, give yourself and your opponent room to breathe and to say 'no.' On such occasions usually there is far more time and space than your impulsiveness and needs would have you believe.

Brannan: Let us turn now to the last ring, the Fifth Circle.

Gresser: Ring 5 is called "After Presentation," and presents a great challenge to a player's integrity. If you commit to another person, Ring 5 requires that you work diligently in carrying out your commitments. If you receive a 'no' in Ring 4, you must decide in Ring 5 whether you will accept the 'no' and abandon your negotiation, or whether to continue in spite of it. Even if the other side accepts your presentation, you may still conclude that you do not wish to proceed.

**RING 5
AFTER
PRESENTATION**

Most players incorrectly assume that simply because a proposal or a presentation has been accepted or an agreement has been reached (i.e., a 'yes'), that the game has ended. In fact often the real play, the hidden negotiation, is about to begin.

There are four basic questions to ask yourself in Ring 5:

- Do I wish to proceed or shall I exercise my own right (i.e., a 'no') to discontinue the play?
- If I decide to begin, what actions can I immediately undertake to help the other party?
- If I have received a 'no,' what actions are now open to me?
- If I decide to proceed in spite of a 'no,' how will this advance my mission?

The key qualities you can cultivate in Ring 5 are modesty and humility which lead to trainability, which we have already discussed. The word "humility" comes from the Latin, "humus," meaning "earth." When we stay close to the earth we can adjust with remarkable agility.

MODESTY AND HUMILITY

There is a sequence in many negotiations which resembles combat: I move (action). You respond. I counter. If you can hold steady in the face of your opponent's responsive move, you will control the game and keep the initiative. The determining factor will be your ability to remain loose, light and free. Ring 5 is a marvelous training of this skill.

In Ring 5 the spotlight is upon the circularity of a negotiation, indeed, of the life process itself. If you view a "negotiation" as an unfolding opportunity to practice and to refine your integrity, the negotiation never ends. There is always a new mountain to climb, a new stream to ford, always more work to be done. This is why the last hexagram in the *I Ching*, the Chinese Book of Changes, is entitled "Before Completion."

The default moves in Ring 5 are straightforward.

If the response to your presentation in Ring 4 is a 'no,' you must now decide what to do—whether to continue to play or not. The first step is to return to Ring 1, examine your original mission and budget, and assess the amount of budget you have expended up to this point. Again, the key is to be **conscious** about your decision, so that it is based on what you want, your mission and your budget. If you decide to continue to play, you may wish to begin in Rings 3 and 4, laying an even stronger foundation for your next presentation.

If the response in Ring 4 is affirmative, you must decide if you wish to continue the game, in other words, to give the other players what they want. Remember, you always have a right to say 'no'—to decide, upon reflection, not to continue.

If you decide to proceed, your task is to work as diligently as you can. By entering your opponents' world and focusing upon what pains them, you will greatly strengthen your own integrity.

In every case, Ring 5 ultimately redirects you back to Ring 1 and requires you to refine your original mission in the light of experience, to become even clearer about what you truly want, how you will arrive there, and the price you must pay.

Brannan:	Julian, in a nutshell can you summarize The Five Rings?
Gresser:	The Five Rings offers a disciplined, orderly process for analyzing the flow of decisions. Each circle creates an opening to develop integrity through the practice of the five core values. Instantly we can know where we are, how we got there, and where to go next. We are always in the game even when we fall out of it. We practice with little things, the incremental steps by which character is built, so when challenges suddenly appear, we are ready. We even want the taste of them.

III. Light and Shadow

"I have no parents. I make heaven and earth my parents.
I have no home. I make awareness my home.
I have no life or death. I make breath tides my life and death.
I have no divine power. I make integrity my divine power.
I have no means. I make understanding my means.
I have no body. I make endurance my body.
I have no eyes. I make the lightning flash my eyes.
I have no ears. I make sensibility my ears.
I have no limbs. I make promptness my limbs.
I have no strategy. I make unshadowed-by-thought my strategy.
I have no designs. I make opportunity my design.
I have no miracles. I make right action my miracles.
I have no principles. I make adaptability my principle.
I have no tactics. I make emptiness/fullness my tactics.
I have no friends. I make you, mind, my friend(s).
I have no enemy. I make carelessness my enemy.
I have no armor. I make compassion my armor.
I have no castle. I make heaven/earth my castle.
I have no sword. I make absence of self my sword."

— 14th century samurai

III. LIGHT AND SHADOW

Brannan: Julian, you have outlined a structure of decision making and effective negotiation, which you call The Five Rings. I think the time has come to link the method to the principal theme of piloting through chaos, and this brings us to the core skills.

Gresser: If our entire enterprise has one purpose, that can be condensed into one principle—integrity—all techniques are contained in one core skill—one noble tactic—and that is Presence. I call this practice "building the container."

But first an introductory comment on chaos itself. Most people associate "chaos" with randomness, discord or turbulence. This is its modern meaning in physics. But if one returns to the original meaning, one doesn't find these elements in the definition. Chaos derives from the Greek word of the same name, which meant, "gape" or space; in other words, the void. Now these terms, over time, have incorporated value judgments that connote trouble or danger. For example, in the Christian literature chaos is seen as the instinctive enemy of order, as Pandemonium, the City of Lucifer, or as the abyss, the frightful domain of witches and trolls. Because of such awful associations we have come to believe that the abyss must be filled up, the gap spanned, and the primordial forces of nature controlled. None of this, as I say, was part of the original meaning. Really, it was value-neutral, simply the void—absolute emptiness.

The original meaning leads us to a rather interesting insight, which the ancient Chinese sages also understood well: The abyss, in its emptiness, contains

THE ORIGINAL MEANING OF CHAOS

all things. It contains danger, but it also contains opportunity. The Chinese character for "crisis" (weiji) is written by combining in a single character the ideographs for danger and opportunity, suggesting that these two coexist and are coequal in every moment. Shakespeare also understood this principle when he wrote, "Sweet are the uses of adversity." But Shakespeare never tells us why adversity is sweet or how to turn it into opportunity. Shall I demonstrate how through the practice of presence adversity can become sweet, right now?

Brannan: Yes, please do.

Gresser: Okay. Let's begin with our friend and colleague, Paula Fox, who is here with us today. Paula, you're a businesswoman, can you describe a situation that is causing you great uneasiness or concern—one in which you can see chaos beginning to lap at your feet?

Ms. Fox: Yes, unfortunately it's only too easy. Tomorrow I'm
BUILDING   going on a business trip to the East Coast where I will
THE CONTAINER meet two colleagues. One of the men is very easygoing, no problem. But the other is a bear. What particularly gripes me is how pushy he is, how he always wants things his way, talks incessantly, and then insists on going out to dinner together. I'm really torn. The project is very important. A lot is riding on it. I don't want to offend him or have a scene. I don't want to make an enemy. But at the same time I really don't want to spend my dinners with this person. Actually I like sitting in my hotel room after a ten-hour day, watching television, relaxing and ordering room service. I am worried about this situation. I am apprehensive about the meeting and, quite frankly, I'm really not looking forward to the trip.

Gresser: Very good. Now, Paula, what I'd like you to do is simply to bring your attention into your body. Okay? Then sketch in your mind an awful but likely scenario that might occur in—where was it?

Ms. Fox: Boston.

Gresser: Okay. Boston. Really allow your imagination to run wild. Terrify yourself and once you really are feeling ghastly, if you would, give us a report of what starts to happen inside of you. Just close your eyes. Shall we begin?

Ms. Fox: (Speaking with her eyes closed) Okay. I arrive. We spend the day together and I feel exhausted and suffocated. Joe suggests we have dinner. I decline. He insists. I say I don't want to. He makes some snide comment. I feel bad. He presses me. There's a blowup. We're not on speaking terms. Then a real mistake occurs. Somebody didn't pay attention and the contract is lost and I'm blamed.

Gresser: Perfect! How do you feel in your body about this scenario?

Ms. Fox: Awful.

Gresser: Splendid!

Can you be a bit more descriptive?

Ms. Fox: My heart is fluttering, I feel angry, this is so unnecessary! I have a constricted feeling around my throat as though I can't breathe. My chest and neck and stomach are tight, and I have indigestion.

Gresser: Marvelous! Now just relax. What I would like you to do is to bring your awareness into your body and simply report to us how you're feeling. For example, if you start to feel frightened, just report the feeling or the emotion and then how it materializes in your body. If you feel angry, just note your anger and the accompanying physical sensations.

You don't have to change or suppress anything. Just attend. You are the witness, the observer of the movie that's beginning. How do you feel about proceeding in this way?

Ms. Fox: I feel fine. It seems interesting.

Gresser: Okay. Continue attending and watch what is happening.

Ms. Fox: (A minute or so elapses. She quietly watches her movie.)

Gresser: Anything special going on?

Ms. Fox: No.

Gresser: Good. Just keep your consciousness in your body. Just relax, let go, and attend.

(A few minutes later)

Ms. Fox: Well, my breathing is settling down a bit now, and my heart is not racing so much.

Gresser: Fine . . . anything else?

Ms. Fox: Let's see . . . my stomach feels better . . . more settled. The tightness around my neck and chest is relieving some and my hands are starting to warm up.

Gresser: Paula, you're doing very well. Just hold steady and keep attending in your body and relax. (A little later. In this practice it is necessary to open some space and be patient for the changes.)

Ms. Fox: The tension is **really** beginning to break up! I feel freer and lighter. I have the sense of collecting power and energy. I'm not quite sure why the situation got me so down. All I really have to do is just tell Joe in a nice way that I'm exhausted. I see how to handle this situation now. It all seems quite simple.

Gresser: Very good, but before you move back into the Thought Tower in your head, just shuttle back into your body and keep checking out what's happening. Do you notice anything else?

Ms. Fox: I have a lot more energy, I mean, **a lot more**. I feel great! Tingling. (She laughs) This is great!

Gresser: (Turning to Tod Brannan) It may be helpful to summarize what has happened here in just a few minutes. First, Paula was very apprehensive and fearful, and her anxieties were beginning to breed even more exaggerated pictures and images. A true runaway catastrophe was in the making. All of this, of course, is in her head. Simply by becoming the observer, by watching how her fears were surfacing in her body (and by watching herself watching herself!) Paula began to get a grip and to restore integrity. And the more she attended to the **physical expression** of her emotions in her body, the more—and this is the beginning of the miracle—the physical sensations and the emotions themselves began to transform. And then later her snapshot of this sliver of reality, which is colored by her emotions and the images created by the emotions, also began to change, and she seemed lighter, younger, and more alive.

             Is that not so, Paula?

Ms. Fox: Yes, that's true. That's what happened.

Gresser: This in essence is our practice. We attend fully to each moment—to each moment with its special dignity. And suddenly things begin to change and we begin to change and there is an opening—a little opening in the darkness, a little glimmer of light. Churchill once remarked, "We create the interior, then it creates us."

Brannan: Very interesting, Julian. Help us understand some of the practical ways to use this technique of "building the container."

Gresser: When we are frightened and helpless, Fear decouples us from our body. By becoming present in our body, we restore the connection.

Fear, like jealousy, is green-eyed and mocks the meat upon which it feeds. Thus Fear makes little and private things, as in Paula's case, great and momentous. And when Panic occupies the stage, no other player has a chance. The practice of Presence holds the line and reminds us who we really are. It is very hard for our grandiose fears to take over when we are truly present.

The practice applies not only in the troughs but also at the crests of life. When things are going really well and we are jubilant, that can be a point of particular vulnerability, because now we have expectations and grow inflated and arrogant. At the crest we are in peril because we are unconscious. The practice of working with the darkness is enormously useful because it helps us hold integrity when we begin to come into the light. It reminds us of the importance of *gravitas*, of steadiness, focus and follow-through. In some sense it requires greater character to continue modestly at the height of success than under the spur of necessity.

But there is another subtlety to the practice, which I

can introduce by way of an old Chinese story, probably from the late 5th and early 6th century A.D.

Brannan: Yes, please do.

Gresser: Two sages were once together. "Where are you going?" asks the elder.

"I am wandering the world at random," replies the younger man.

"And what do you think of wandering?" the patriarch inquires.

"I do not know," responds the younger.

"Not knowing is most intimate," the elder man observes.

Most intimate—this is the great secret. When Fear comes up, as in Paula's case, the fear of what an uncertain situation might hold, we can settle down to find peace and intimacy with ourself in the mists of not-knowing. For it is in the mists that we make our discoveries, as she has done.

This ability to be at ease in not-knowing is also one of the links to true creativity. Keats once wrote:

NEGATIVE CAPABILITY

"It struck me what quality went to form a Man of Achievement, especially in literature, and which Shakespeare possessed so enormously—I mean, **Negative Capability**, that is, when a man is capable of being in uncertainties, mysteries, and doubts, without any irritable reaching after fact and reason."

This **no irritable reaching** after fact and reason holds a clue not only to creative expression in the arts, it is also the mark of the martial artist and of the great negotiators. For when you are loose and light, your heart open and your body peaceful and happy, the openings—especially in the darkness—come to you, and in legions when you least expect them, and then resistance gives way.

Brannan: The concept of Negative Capability seems very important as a literary skill. But what is its greatest test in the field of negotiation? Where does the rubber really meet the road?

Gresser: I would say around issues of time. Perhaps the greatest point of vulnerability in any Ring is when we lose our sense of connection, believing that we're out of time. The dynamic is clear: We feel a sense of urgency, this produces need, need churns and upsets the emotions, consciousness is dispersed, we begin to panic, we act impulsively, which usually produces an untoward result and only aggravates our sense of crisis. Do you remember Flanagan? He could have panicked, seeing all the months of preparation fly out the window. But he held. He did not reach for a closing or even certainty. Actually you remember he turned the time-need dynamic around on his Japanese hosts by using the Sword of Silence. It was they who couldn't stand the slowdown in the pace, it was they who needed to reach irritably both on the second day and in the weeks following after fact, reason and certainty.

I have seen this time-need issue in many international and domestic negotiations. Right now I have a client, a semiconductor company in Los Angeles, which is negotiating a technology-development agreement with a huge German conglomerate. Every time the president of this company jumps the gun out of need (ignoring what he has learned) and impulsively asks for confirmation or spills information, the Germans pull away. Every time he holds together around time issues, resists the impulse to make a phone call or to send a fax, the Germans call or approach him in a welcoming way. It's a fascinating demonstration of the "dance" of integrity in full-motion video.

Brannan: Are there other tests?

Gresser: As your skill advances, the tests get harder. The more conscious you become, the more painful it is to be unconscious. But then you must have compassion when you fail. The next step is to be generous to one-self, and to know that often, when we are most per-plexed, it is at that moment that the angels of our better nature walk through the door. It is then that the miracle happens.

Brannan: How can we prepare for such things?

Gresser: By *gravitas*. Someone once asked Coleridge, "How can angels fly?" And he answered him, "Because they take themselves lightly." The more present and rooted we are, the less encumbered by vanity, the easier for our spirits to soar. The practice is straightforward. Track five times this week when you have felt overwhelmed, shuttled into your body and attended to what was hap-pening. Then track five times this week when you allowed your fears to overwhelm you. Then a third case: When your fears appeared and you started to succumb, note five times you exercised your Will, entered into your body, and like Odysseus and the Sirens, held onto the mast of being present, and observed what magic happened then.

We are dealing with deeply-rooted, early pathways of behavior, and of these the programming of Fear from childhood seems the most entrenched. We must be patient with ourselves. Steadiness and practice is everything.

Zuigan, a great master, used to remind himself to be present throughout each day.

"Master, Master," he would say.

"Yes, yes," would be his reply.

"Thoroughly awake?" he would inquire.

"Yes, yes," would be his response.

"Don't be deceived by others," he would warn himself.

"No, no," he would respond.

This "Don't be deceived by others," refers not only to the external world. It refers also to the inner—to our fears, conceits, and dilemmas, to our sense of helplessness that wastes our powers, that pulls us from our true connection, our line to the way things really are, which is our integrity.

Brannan: The story of Zuigan suggests that staying awake may be the key.

Gresser: Yes, staying awake. And what things we can discover when we are awake! How beautiful and plentiful and filled with hope this world really is.

I would like to focus now upon the techniques of discovery, because it is fair to say that every step in a negotiation creates an opening for ourselves and other players upon the stage which is the world. The great negotiators are all explorers and discoverers.

Brannan: Okay.

Gresser: The first principle of discovery is No Assumptions, No Expectations, which perhaps you remember is also

NO ASSUMPTIONS/ the second core value. Assumptions and expectations
NO EXPECTATIONS and the hunger that drives them impair our ability
to see things as they truly are. The stronger the
hunger, the greater the distortion. Thus we are interested in what Leonardo da Vinci called, *saper vedere*,
how to see.

Brannan: Are you suggesting that even seeing is a skill and that
most people do not know how to see?

Gresser: I am. Virtually all of us live in a semi-trance and our
society enforces a consensus on reality. I say, "Accept
my version of reality, and **I'll** go along with **yours**."
And so we become deadened and succumb.

One of the most dramatic examples of consensus
trance is the first entry of Captain Cook's ship, the
Endeavor, into Botany Bay, Australia. "There she was,"
writes Alan Moorehead in his wonderful book, *The*
CONSENSUS   *Fatal Impact*, with her high masts and her great sails,
TRANCE   and then she passed within a quarter of a mile of some
fisherman in four canoes. They did not even bother
to look up. Then when she had anchored close to the
shore, a naked woman carrying wood appeared with
three children. She often looked at the ship, but
expressed neither surprise nor concern. Soon after
this she lighted a fire, and the four canoes came in
from the fishing. The people landed, hauled up
their boats and began to dress for dinner, to all
appearance totally unmoved by us . . ."

"But later when small boats were put to shore, the
natives raised a great alarm, recognizing the sailors as
human, although a palpable evil with their odd clothes
and pale faces. The first sight of the *Endeavor* had
apparently meant nothing to these people, because
it was **too** strange, too monstrous to be compre-
hended. It appeared out of nowhere like some men-
acing phenomenon of nature, a water spout or a roll

of thunder, and by ignoring it or pretending to ignore it, no doubt the natives hoped it would go away."

Psychologists call it a negative hallucination. We become so inured, so clubbed down, that the mind no longer trusts and refuses to process what the senses report, and the only thing that is real is what is tried and familiar.

You might think it implausible that consensus trance occurs every day in business.

Brannan: It would seem implausible but let's have an example.

Gresser: I will give you a modern example of consensus trance.

I was once training a group of executives in their Japanese negotiations. "What is it you want?" I asked one of them.

"I want our Japanese joint venture partner to invest more money in the venture," he instantly replied.

"Fine. Now, what is it you **really** want?" I pressed him.

"I just told you." He was somewhat nonplussed.

"What do you **really** want?" I repeated . . . "if you were to drop all your assumptions about what is not possible."

"I can't think of anything else," he replied.

"It's okay, take your time," I said. You have to be gentle with people when they go into the discovery mode.

"Nothing else is coming up," he said, a little impatiently.

Five minutes passed, then ten minutes. Some people in the workshop were becoming uneasy. Remember Flanagan? Unlike Flanagan, these people were not trained. They were unused to silence. Finally the executive blurted out, "All right, you've pushed me hard. What I really want is to take over my joint venture partner. That's what I want. But you know it's **impossible**! No foreigner can ever take over a Japanese company, **you know** that."

"I've been involved in several takeovers."

"What! You can do that?!! Well, if that were **really** possible—and I'm **very** skeptical—that's what I **really** want."

And so on. Somehow he seemed to have physically grown larger in his chair, become brighter and more alive. And all that had really changed was that he had put aside the crutch, the belief which had served him too well and too long, that what he really wanted was quite impossible.

Gresser: I will give you another example, a French case that grounds the move of "no assumptions" in an even more real-life business setting.

The president of a major American electronics manufacturer faced a dilemma over his company's joint venture. On one hand, he felt duty-bound to uphold an oral promise to invest $5 million in the French joint venture company. On the other, he had a vague, uneasy feeling—not so much about the investment itself, but about his French partner's real intentions. A $5 million investment would not be an excessive burden if it would help the venture grow and prosper. But the joint venture company had never been profitable since beginning operations in the mid-1980s, and the American president was not even sure how important profitability was to his French partner. Then too, increasingly, his French partner was pressuring him to transfer core manufacturing and other know-how to France.

If the French partner simply intended to use the joint venture as a vehicle to acquire critical technology, the American president was clear that he would not be interested in transferring manufacturing operations to France, nor would he want to go through with the $5 million investment, nor even to encourage in any way the joint venture's further development. The problem was how to discover his French partner's real agenda?

Being a man of the world, the first thing the American president did was to take stock of instances in which his own integrity and that of his core team had been upheld or compromised. He observed that he and his colleagues had developed a vested interest (a **need**) **not** to see. They had become so imbued by their own desires and hopes for the joint venture, with what it would do for **them**, that it never really occurred to him to look deeply into the concerns or motivations of the French partner. Embedded in his own needs and desires were a number of critical assumptions about the nature of the venture itself. Basically, the American president had been assuming all along that his French partner naturally shared his hope that the joint venture would flourish. The American president also assumed that his company had actually entered into a "partnership" in the American sense of the term (e.g., a fiduciary relationship), and that the joint venture itself naturally was the owner, not the French parent, of all technology transferred to it under a license.

This was not how his French counterparts perceived the venture. They did not view themselves as "partners" in any way, except when they made use of the delusion of the Americans to serve their own interests. The senior executives in the French parent company felt entitled to all the technology in the venture. Although the license clearly specified that all technology transferred was solely the property of the joint venture, the key French managers believed it only "fair" that the parent company should be able to use the technology because of its substantial equity investment and loan guarantees to the venture.

While engaging in this process of self-reflection, the American president began to scrutinize significant lapses or mismatches between the behavior of his French partner and the stated purpose of both parties to the joint venture. The first thing he noted was a curious lack of interest on the French side in making the joint venture profitable. For example, despite protests by the Americans, no plans of any sort had been prepared to realize the goal of profitability. The American president began to pay more careful attention than he had in the past to the kinds of questions the French parties were asking at all levels of this company—questions about patents, about technical problems, about bottlenecks in their solutions, many questions quite outside the ordinary ambit of concerns of the joint venture. He began to receive strange reports, which he had hitherto largely ignored, for example, the discovery late one evening of a French engineer faxing sensitive information back to the French parent company. This engineer had been recruited from the U.S. company's chief competitor by the French Chairman of the Board of the joint venture, and then seconded to work at the U.S. company in California.

A clear picture began to emerge of the incompatibility of the French mission with the expectations and hopes of the Americans. The pattern became so clear, it seemed a face peering out across the many months in which the two companies had operated together.

Using the yardstick of integrity, the American president asked himself, "Why should we invest $5 million in a joint venture in which our French partner appears to be operating on an entirely different mission, one which is incompatible with our own?" Without accusation or recrimination the American president quietly resolved not to invest further in the joint venture and looked for other more exciting opportunities in Europe.

The key to "winning" this negotiation was the American president's determination to reclaim his integrity (the "inner negotiation"). This occurred when he began to distance himself from his "needs," and at last truly to listen. At this point he started to uncover all sorts of unnoticed "facts" directly pertinent to the critical issues before him. He began to challenge his own assumptions and to look with fresh eyes at what was really going on. He paid particular attention to instances where integrity in his company was being violated and when it was upheld. And as he probed deeply, he discovered his French partner's true agenda, which had been "obvious" all along in the flux of events, conditions and circumstances. Without engaging in "mind-reading" he reached an **effective decision** that ultimately saved his company millions of dollars and years of wasted effort.

When we allow ourselves to come in touch, to see what might be possible just underneath the surface, what a transformation occurs! Until he became willing to challenge his assumptions, the American president in the French joint venture was content to move blithely towards a disastrous investment, the student in the seminar could not imagine taking over a Japanese company, the villagers could not conceive that it was possible to cross the reefs by means of a canoe. Simply to allow ourselves **the chance to see** will affect the probabilities that what we see happens.

The method of how to see is straightforward. Anyone can learn it with only a little practice. The first step is to identify and to write down succinctly what you **believe** you want. Next, identify any assumptions you are making about what is impossible. Look for assumptions that crib your ability to see. Drop these assumptions. Put them aside, even when they pull at you. Then rephrase what you want. Look for a fresh way to express it. We want our emotions and our creative imagination, which are always curious about novelty, to express themselves.

Finally, see if you can stretch a little more. This "little more" is where often real discovery begins. When we were children we played in a sea of wishes, for in the mind's eye of a child everything is possible. We want to recapture this original innocence.

I have found in my life, Tod, that when we drop our assumptions and expectations, put them aside like old and tattered clothes, suddenly we are less burdened and more alive. Each moment presents itself, in all its freshness, and we are free.

Brannan: Your example illustrates one of the uses of no assumptions in identifying what we really want. Are there other tactical uses?

Gresser: I will give you a very advanced example which illustrates how Presence and No Assumptions work together. I am before a client and we are discussing his dealings with Japan. Suddenly I start to feel fear, a tingling along my forearms, a bristling on the hairs of my neck. My heart is beating faster. "Why am I feeling afraid?" I say to myself, "There is no cause for fear.

Yet here is fear! Might I be assuming anything? Let me see." I pause and think for a moment. My client observes none of this internal dialogue.

"Well, look at this! I am assuming this is **my** fear, my anxiety. This '**mine**' is the problem. Let me drop 'mine' and see what I can see. It is not mine at all. It seems it is **his** fears, yes, look at the quiver under his eyes, how he holds himself. Fear has crept into the room. Even the walls now seem to shudder."

Like a tranquil lake, our body/mind can pick up even the most subtle perturbations of some passing breeze.

When we develop *gravitas* our mind can discern all sorts of strange things in the field, and the clearer we are, the clearer the mirror becomes. This is one of the tactical uses of equanimity and compassion.

This technique of No Assumptions, No Expectations, is celebrated in some of the classic Japanese *chambara* (samurai) movies. I don't know if you have ever seen the movie, *The Seven Samurai*, by Akira Kurosawa. The story is a simple one. A village is threatened by brigands. A group of seven samurai comes to its aid, but in the ensuing battle all but two are killed. In one of the early scenes, the archer, the elder statesman of the group (who survives) seeks to recruit a masterless warrior (*rōnin*) to the cause. He devises a way to test the degree of skill of the candidate. A young man who aspires to join the band is planted behind the door with a stick. His instructions are to attack anyone who passes through the entry.

The street is busy with the traffic of merchants and geisha, petty officials and tatami makers. From time to time a *rōnin* passes by. The archer hails him. The *rōnin* approaches, smiles and enters through the doorway. The young man attacks but he is easily repelled. "Very fine!" the archer compliments the *rōnin*. But the *rōnin* is insulted at the impudence of being tested and leaves in a huff. Several other candidates appear, but for financial and other reasons, all refuse.

Finally, just as the archer and his comrades are about to give up, a samurai appears at the threshold. He pauses. Something is amiss. Perhaps a physical sensation or merely a shadow crosses his mind. We do not know. Then he laughs—a great belly laugh. Ha! Ha! Ha! He sees and understands. How amusing! He is the man the archer has been looking for! No assumptions, no expectations, the true martial artist.

The story embodies the true spirit of the samurai: "I have no means, I make understanding my means. I have no eyes, I make the lightning flash my eyes. I have no tactics, I make emptiness/fullness my tactics."

Brannan: This seems a prescription for combat but can it apply equally to a negotiation?

Gresser: The same. I will show you. Let's turn to tactics. In particular, one tactic, the question.

Most people believe that you ask a question to obtain information.

Brannan: Yes, most people believe that.

Gresser: Yet there is another, more interesting use of questions and that is to facilitate discovery. Each step in a negotiation is an opportunity to discover something singular about ourselves and our opponents: "What is this? I don't know. Let me see . . ." The steady, curious mind is the negotiator's mind. So it follows that telling is rarely negotiating . . ." "You should know that . . ." How many people will accept what you tell

THE QUESTION

them? We live in an age of sceptics. Asking rather than telling, letting the eye of discovery open, that is a much better practice.

Brannan: Let's return for a moment to basics. When you speak of discovery questions, what precisely do you mean?

Gresser: There are two kinds of questions. The first is the inter-rogatory—'who,' 'how,' 'what,' 'why,' 'where,' 'when.'

THE BRUSH   I call the interrogatory the "brush," because with a single sweep you can help another person see the entire canvas. The second are verb-led questions—'do,' 'can,' 'should,' 'will,' 'may,' and so forth. I call this form, the "scalpel," because it is useful in deli-cate conceptual surgery. Because verb-led questions invite really only three possible answers—'yes,' 'no,' and 'maybe'—their range of discovery can be quite limited.

Brannan: What are the consequences of using one form of ques-tion or another?

Gresser: The important point is to understand the relation-ship of the **form** of the question to "need." An untrained player will often fall into the trap of begin-ning an interview with a verb-led question—"Are you pleased with our new product line . . ." How much discovery does this question invite? "Yes, we are." "No, we're not . . ." Or equivocally, "Yes, we are, but not really, because . . ."

An untrained player will see a 'no' as a rejection or as a sign of failure. A 'maybe' will also be unsettling. As I said before, in the West we have been pro-grammed from when we were very young to feel a need for resolution (agreement) and to fear uncer-tainty. There is much "irritable reaching," as Keats put it, after fact and reason. Therefore I recommend to beginners, open an encounter with the "brush,"

"What are the great challenges you face in your work … In your highest hopes where do you see your enterprise by the year 2000?" and so forth. I ask of my students no more than I ask of myself, to be wary of the impulse, the lunge for fact and certainty, which is embodied in the verb-led question.

Brannan: What are the uses of the "scalpel"?

Gresser: Microsurgery. "Is the dot on the butterfly's wing pale green?" "Will you marry me?"

THE SCALPEL   But again, the "scalpel" is not for the faint-of-heart. "Will you marry me?" How many young men have spent years of precious budget, time and effort, financial reserves, and their most creative emotions on the horns of this 'maybe.' And I have seen over the years the same behavior with countless desperate foreign executives seeking a 'yes' from their elusive Japanese opponents.

Brannan: In business can you give an example of how to use the two kinds of questions in opening the discovery process?

Gresser: Selling is a common situation. In selling, your task is to help the prospective purchaser discover how the benefits incorporated into your mission can solve his (or her) pain. (The reader may want to review at this point the discussion of mission and purpose.) The first step I recommend is to take a "snapshot" in your mind of the discovery you want the other player to make. Here is how to do this:

- First find the pain.
- Next connect the pain to the benefits you bring.
- Finally wrap the benefits into an interrogatory question.

For example. Suppose I am planning a workshop with some colleagues in London. Our target is the legal counsel of large European companies. We want to feature the applications of The Five Rings process in international negotiations and alternative dispute settlements. My associates in London tell me that European lawyers, like their American counterparts, are under terrific pressure to save money for their companies and to handle their overwhelming case load more effectively. Also, they are continuously harassed by senior management, who generally are not lawyers, don't care about the subtleties of the law, and want "results."

Once we begin to understand the "pain" of the general counsel, the next step is to connect the pain to the greatest benefits we convey, either by our cause, our product, our service, our person, organization, and so forth.

In this case it occurs to me, these general counsel do not possess a skill-based system that will enable them to conserve budget and help them deal more effectively with their own senior management. By "system," I refer to a measurable way of instantly correcting errors or repeating successes and a process that helps us do this with ever-increasing skill.

If I were before one of these general counsel (the same text might also be adapted to advertising copy) I might begin as follows. Here is what the dialogue with General Counsel could look like:

Gresser: "What are some of the toughest issues you are facing today in your job?"

Counsel: "Tight budgets and pressure from senior management."

Gresser:	"What kind of headway are you making in settling cases more efficiently?"
Counsel:	"So-so. We do well with some, not so well with others."
Gresser:	"And with your top management."
Counsel:	"That's a continuing headache."
Gresser:	"A continuing headache. . .how?"

(Once a player expresses some pain, you need to follow up with a second interrogatory—in this case, **how.**)

Counsel:	"They don't understand. They expect everything yesterday."
Gresser:	"How much cost saving does your top management want over the next year?"
Counsel:	"At least 10%."
Gresser:	"Did I hear you say 10%?"
Counsel:	"Yes."
Gresser:	"What about 20% or 30%?"
Counsel:	"They would be ecstatic, but it's impossible."
Gresser:	"When you speak of cost saving, what are you specifically referring to?"
Counsel:	"Pounds saved."
Gresser:	"But what about time and creativity? How do you go about conserving these elements?"
Counsel:	"We really don't pay much attention to them."

Gresser:	"I see. In addition to saving money, how important might it be for you also to conserve time, so that you can focus your creativity on what is most important to you?"
Counsel:	"It would be great, but how would you go about it?"
Gresser:	"There is a way. We can come to that in a moment if you like. But let me ask you, if I may, what **system** do you have today to achieve significant additional levels of cost saving?"
Counsel:	"I beg your pardon?"
Gresser:	"What **system** do you possess today to achieve not only 10%, but possibly even 20% or 30%, in the areas we are discussing?"
	(NOTE: It is general good practice to stay close to the original question, without changing the language. If you change the language of the question, you will alter slightly the discovery. Just relax, hold integrity and observe.)
Counsel:	"I guess we don't have a system" (the basic discovery).
Gresser:	"We may be able to help you on this one. . . when was the last "win" you had with your senior management?"
Counsel:	"What do you mean by "win"?"
Gresser:	"A time when you felt you negotiated effectively and came away having achieved your mission and feeling good and clean about yourself—a time you knew for sure you were doing a good job and being of service to your company and the world."
Counsel:	"I don't know. I don't remember."

Gresser:	"We have a way to help you if you are interested . . ."
Counsel:	"I am interested. Show me."
	And so forth.
	Now this is just an overview, but I wanted to give you the flavor.
	Can you see? There is little telling, much asking, mainly using the "brush," trying to explore and to understand that general counsel's world, always asking oneself as we proceed: "How can I help? Where is his or her dilemma? Can I really fix it?"
Brannan:	Isn't **how** one asks a question as important as the substance of the question itself?
Gresser:	You are quite right. And that brings me to the subject of "nurturing." The greater our integrity, the
NURTURING	more we are able to nourish ourselves and others. Generosity of spirit comes naturally to us. We feel abundant and our cup overflows. And yet, when dealing with others, sometimes it is necessary to have a touch of the coyote.
Brannan:	What do you mean?
Gresser:	It may be a perversity of human nature that most people feel better (okay) about themselves when another person is not quite okay, and slightly diminished (not okay) by the good fortune of others.
Brannan:	Oh, come on. That is a pretty cynical view of the world.
Gresser:	No, I don't think so. Someone hears that a friend in the same line of work has just obtained a great reward or benefit. How does that person feel? Wonderful, of course, at his friend's success. But in his voice, if

you listen carefully, you can detect a note of sadness, even envy. The voice says, "Why not I? Am **I** not as good? Why should not I also enjoy such benefits?" Another person hears of her friend's misfortune. Her husband has run off with another woman. She meets her friend and commiserates. Listen carefully. In her voice of consolation there is a note of glee! "Thank God it is not I," she tells herself. She feels relieved and a little better.

NOT-OKAY-ON-PURPOSE

Here's the point. In the practice of integrity, we generally want to make room for the other person to feel okay by becoming slightly not-quite-okay-on-purpose. This is particularly useful around pain. When a person is struggling with something painful, the process of discovery naturally shuts down. After all, most people have not been trained to "hold" steady, to be open and present to their pain. So your task is to create the container that will hold their pain, and often one element in the process is for you to be **not-okay**. It takes much containment to have the sense of humor to be **not-okay-on-purpose**.

Brannan:

Sounds pretty manipulative and tricky to me.

Gresser:

It can be. If nurturing comes solely out of tactics and is motivated simply to gain advantage, it degenerates into manipulation, and you will pay a heavy price in your integrity for playing the coyote.

But when nurturing comes out of abundance and a recognition that we must allow and build an opening for discovery, then it has a solid base and it can be grounded in integrity. I believe there are both Western and Eastern archetypes and stories that reinforce what I am saying. Odysseus, the most crafty and resourceful of all men, was also a man of noble character. Abraham Lincoln, a man of seemingly inexhaustible compassion, was also sly and crafty as a fox.

Both Odysseus and Abraham Lincoln deeply understood human frailty.

I should also like to point out the clear relationship between **not-okay-on-purpose** and managing **need**. Most people **need** to be okay, **need** to feel better than their fellows, so it is quite a good exercise to practice becoming comfortable with just being wrong, not okay, or looking silly and uninformed. Try it. It is not easy. I am not saying make me your fool, simply that it often is useful to adopt what the martial arts schools refer to as the "low stance."

For those who feel uncomfortable with the idea of purposely adopting a pose of being not-okay, a little story may be helpful.

It is said that after the death of the great master Hakuin, a visitor approached a blind man who was sitting before the temple where the master used to teach. "Tell me about Hakuin," the visitor asked the blind man.

"He was a very special person," the blind man began, adjusting his position on his begging mat. "When most people hear about the misfortune of a friend, I can detect in their voice, along with the sorrow, a note of happiness. And when they learn of the good fortune of another, I can hear sadness behind their happiness. It was never so with Hakuin. When he heard of another's misfortune, you could hear in his voice only sadness and when he learned of another's good fortune I can remember only happiness. There was no distance."

As our integrity increases, the "distance" between ourselves and the other closes, until like Hakuin there is no distance at all, and tactics are no longer necessary. In the meantime it is good practice to do what we can to put the other person at ease in order to facilitate discovery.

Brannan: You have been describing situations where we ask the questions. Suppose our opponent starts to ask us questions? How do we respond?

Gresser: The key point to remember is that you can always say 'no.' You don't have to give out a scintilla of information more than you wish to. This brings me to the subject of the "parry" and "reverse."

**PARRY AND
REVERSE**   Think of the "parry" as a connector, i.e., "and..." "I'm not sure..." "I understand..." "Good idea..." "Good question..." "Hmm..." "Well, let me see"..."I want to fully understand what you are saying"... Or sometimes simply pure silence. The connector cuts in both directions. It parries your opponent's questions and it also helps draw out a party who is beginning to divulge information.

The reverse simply repeats a question with a question. Crudely performed, it will be obvious that you are holding back information. Expertly executed, interposing a parry before the reverse, and then struggling, which is a form of being **not-okay-on-purpose**, and the reverse will become invisible! The more the tactic flows out of a sense of presence and timing, the more powerful it is, and the less you or the other party will sense it as being manipulative.

Brannan: How about an example from your practice?

Gresser: Here is a case, again from my experience in Japanese negotiations. The Japanese team arrives with a long and detailed list of technical questions, obviously prepared with great care and thought. Suppose I run a small company which manufactures electroencephalogram equipment. The scene is in my Chicago office. We are in Ring 3—positioning and negotiating the presentation. The dialogue might proceed something like this.

Gresser: "Mr. Honda, I want to commend you for the amount of time you and your staff have devoted to preparing these excellent questions."

Mr. Honda: "Thank you very much, Mr. Gresser. It's a pleasure to meet you."

Gresser: "How can I be of service to you?"

Mr. Honda: "Well, we have only a few questions. May I begin?"

Gresser: "Yes, please do."

Mr. Honda: "Let me see. We do not quite understand why you are using analog circuits to detect the alpha beta brain waves."

Gresser: "Excellent question, Mr. Honda. But frankly I'm really not qualified to be of much help on this one, as I am not an engineer myself. Let me ask Mr. Hartzell, who is here with me." (Mr. Hartzell has gone through extensive training, and will help me in this negotiation as a blocker.)

Mr. Hartzell: "Yes, this is a very good point, Mr. Honda, but it's a complicated question. Let me see. I'm not sure in what respect you're speaking."

Mr. Honda: "We're particularly interested in how you track and set amplitudes and frequencies."

Mr. Hartzell: "Interesting (resisting the impulse to spill). In order for me to be of best use to you, let me understand . . . how could this be helpful to you and your company? (Note the interrogatory coupled with nurturing.) Perhaps I can be more specific. What problem are your engineers struggling with that we might help you address?"

Mr. Honda: "Hmm (somewhat puzzled). I'm not sure (a 'maybe')."

Mr. Hartzell: (Pure silence. Resists the need to fill up the space.)

Mr. Honda: (Returning to the battle) "Well, we are having some difficulty with lag. During EEG measurements with digital circuits . . ."

Mr. Hartzell: "Lag. How interesting. What seems to be the problem?"

And so forth.

Gresser: Who did most of the telling in this negotiation? Who asked most of the questions? Who spilled information? Who held integrity? You will find that the laundry list/fishing expedition style of negotiation can backfire. In fact it is a great liability, because the skillful negotiator who knows how to ask questions and to listen will quickly go upstream to the hidden intention. All you have to do is remain loose, not be afraid to say 'no,' and stay focused on your mission. It's all play once you have the hang of it.

Brannan: Yes, but to develop this sense of fun and play requires, as you say, real steadiness and an ability to stay awake. Are there any moves that build steadiness and alertness right in the thick of things?

Gresser: One useful technique is the "pendulum." See Illustration 3. The question is this: Where should you **THE PENDULUM** "position" yourself, emotionally, when another player (your "opponent") starts to discover and become enthusiastic or excited over what you are saying? This is the first question. The second is, where should you optimally be placed when the emotional pendulum swings the other way, and your opponent begins to doubt, objects or becomes outright negative?

Brannan: I don't have a clue.

Gresser: Well, where do you suppose?

Brannan: I imagine you share your opponents' excitement when they are positive and try to persuade them of the merits of your cause when they are unconvinced.

Gresser: That has not been my experience.

There is a natural tendency, when someone starts to assent, particularly if he (or she) becomes enthusiastic about our proposal, for us also to become excited. Their enthusiasm is infectious, the creative imagination gets to work, and a hundred swirling expectations immediately issue forth. If we do not watch out, soon we are stepping ahead of ourselves. But it is an unstable branch, for just when we start to feel giddy, our opponent will back off, sensing that something must be wrong if we are that excited.

THE PENDULUM

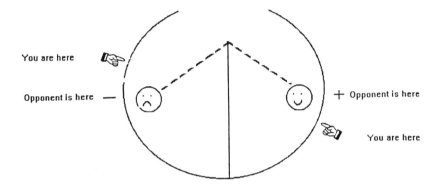

The Pendulum

The chart indicates where, ideally, you should position yourself on the pendulum: When your opponents become excited you can also become enthusiastic, but not as excited as they. When your opponents have doubts, hesitate or become negative, you must acknowledge their concerns and point out that what you are proposing may not be suitable for them.

ILLUSTRATION 3

THE POSITIVE PENDULUM

It is fine to rejoice along with another's discoveries, but our focus should be upon building the container that will hold their and our emotions. The optimal "place," in my experience, is to be positive and curious when our opponent is positive, but not quite as positive as he or she. This is what I call the "positive pendulum."

NOTE: Being "neutral," uninterested or detached, however, will only deflate another player unnecessarily.

THE NEGATIVE PENDULUM

The negative pendulum works in reverse. When things turn dark or negative, our need and impulsiveness will cause us to push back and try to convince the other player to change his (her) mind. A sensitive opponent will become even more disaffected and thereby set up a negative spiral: We become needy, our opponent becomes even more rejecting, we begin to panic, and so forth..Your best shot is not to push back at all—simply get out of the way.

"I don't buy what you're saying," says your opponent. "I'm not sure I'd buy it either," you say. Whoosh! No one's at home! Only empty space. What can the other player do? In most cases out of sheer confusion at such a bizarre response, your opponent will move back toward the positive pole.

And you know, this may be the "right" move, the effective move from the perspective of integrity. . . because you will have signaled that you are a person who respects a 'no' and has a sense of fun, who is patient when things don't go your way, no matter what direction the pendulum swings. That is the kind of person you yourself will want to be associated with.

Brannan: What if the pendulum rests in the doldrums, at dead center?

Gresser: Then you probably must churn the emotions to get the energy moving. Take some contrary and unexpected action. There is nothing like breaking the tedium of convention to stir the pot. As a negotiator I would rather have consciousness in chaos than inertia or unresponsive idleness.

Brannan: Any other tactics you can recommend?

Gresser: Next comes the "Checkpoint." Up till now we have been discussing techniques that facilitate discovery. The Checkpoint and taking notes both facilitate and confirm discovery.

CHECKPOINT   Most people have an agenda, some critical bit of information they hold back, either consciously or unconsciously. Japanese culture, and to a lesser extent other countries of East Asia, place a premium on what is unstated, uncertain, concealed, unexpressed, and silent. Whereas each player has a right to volunteer only as much or as little information as he or she wishes, it may be important for us, in the interest of avoiding making invalid assumptions, to test the discoveries we have made. This is the function of the "Checkpoint." The Checkpoint simply repeats back in the language of the other player what you have heard—repeats it back at least three times.

Brannan: What's so special about the number **3**?

Gresser: Our system is filled with magical numbers: the **5** Rings, the **5** core values (5 being a "power" word, i.e., the first five books of the Bible [Pentateuch] the Pentacost, the Pentagon, etc.), the **4** eyes of integrity—3-in-1—which suggests the divine trinity in unity, and the balance of opposites, 2-on-2. There is also a famous line in Goethe's *Faust,* "The devil knocks thrice!" Less mysteriously, **3** seems sufficient to help get us through the first layers of delusion.

Brannan: Why use the Checkpoint in the first place?

Gresser: Because you want to verify that what you are hearing
                is in fact what is being said. If you fail to do this and
                merrily proceed on your way, you may be greatly sur-
                prised when your opponent challenges you later.
                "That's not what I said. That's not what I meant at
                all."

Brannan: How about an example.

Gresser: A person agrees to invest in your company on what
                appear good terms for everyone. "Bill," you say, "I'm
                delighted at the prospect of your becoming an
                investor, but I just want to make sure this deal is really
                for you. (Checkpoint 1)

                "Yes, Julian," he says, "I'm excited about working
                together." "Great," you say. "We're most happy that
                you feel comfortable with the terms." (Checkpoint 2)

                "Perfectly," he says. "We had a few differences, but I
                think this arrangement will work for everyone."
                "Excellent," you say. "I just wanted to confirm that
                you felt the way we do." (Checkpoint 3)

                The next day perhaps you check once again, "We're
                very pleased to be working together. In fact, there are
                some new opportunities, X, Y and Z, that could be
                very promising." (Checkpoint 4)

                "That's great," says the investor. "I have some ideas I
                also wanted to discuss with you."

                The untrained and needy player will skip over the
                Checkpoint. He will be afraid that the investor will
                renege and, you know, the investor, sensing the need,
                will begin unconsciously to have buyer's remorse. If
                you are not afraid of 'no' and you respect the other

player, you will extend the courtesy of the Checkpoint. My experience suggests that this simple move can bring you closer.

In some cultures, like Japan, you must repeat the Checkpoint more than three times, sometimes five and six, even ten times, to get to the real feelings and to the real intention. (In Japanese, the unstated, deeper sentiment is translated, *honne*, which means literally "basic sound.")

There are many famous stories illustrating how a failure to use the Checkpoint, along with poor translation, has created ludicrous misunderstandings in U.S.-Japanese relations. One case involved the meeting between President Nixon and Prime Minister Sato during negotiations to open Japan's textile market. After hearing President Nixon's urgent request, Prime Minister Sato concluded the meeting with the promise of "*zensho shimasu.*" President Nixon's translator rendered this phrase, "We will do our best," whereupon Nixon returned triumphant. "Japanese concede!" the American headlines puffed. But everyone in Japan understood that *zensho shimasu* means something like, "Well, we'll do our best, but we're very sorry that most likely things won't work. Very sorry that we can't help you out."

A rudimentary use of the Checkpoint would have fleshed out this basic difference in perspectives.

Brannan: Note-taking seems such an innocuous thing. I'm not sure I see why you call it a "tactic."

Gresser: Ah, there is note-taking, and then there is **note-taking**! Note-taking has several generally underestimated uses. First, it helps us focus. Note-taking demands that we listen carefully. The manual act of coordinating eye, hand and ear forces concentration.

Second, we create a record. But this is not an ordinary record. It is a record generated from the eyes of system. "Is this player arrogant?" "How quickly does he reveal emotions?" "How 'trainable' is she?" "What curious things are happening in the ecology of this situation?" Questions such as these contain all the clues, and without note-taking it is hard to recall the nuances.

Finally, note-taking prepares the countermove. Do you remember? Action-response-countermove. Your opponent's reaction to your initiating action will create the opening. Your notes, common sense, and your intuition will guide you to the best next move.

The question now is, in this play and counter-play, where is the mind? Where should the mind be at the point of combat?

Brannan: Combat?

Gresser: Yes, combat. Each point in a negotiation is combat. First and foremost, combat with ourselves—combat with our vanity, our conceits, fears and lethargy, combat with routine and mediocrity. To this also add combat with the blindness, ignorance or viciousness of our opponents.

Tod, where should the mind be?

Brannan: I don't know.

Gresser: Empty mind, open heart (in Japanese and Chinese the character for "mind" and "heart," *shin*, is the same.) A blank slate. Your opponent moves; the move is written down upon the slate. Your opponent speaks; the words are inscribed. An impression, perhaps an idea, comes up; you take note. "What is this?" Nothing else. Quietly you observe, you watch the play.

The Pure Self watches the self. You sense the right moment and you act. When the full conceptual understanding takes form and aligns itself with reason, it is already too late! Here is an example of how far ahead of conceptual understanding is the heart/mind if not obstructed by the ego.

I participated yesterday in a panel in Dallas, Texas, on the theme of negotiating in Asia. We were running late when we began and the head of the conference asked the chairman of our panel to shorten the presentations so that the audience could have time for questions. But the chairman felt he had come a long way and was not about to be restricted, so he spoke for 40-45 minutes, the other two participants went on for about 20-25 minutes each, and when it came time for me to speak, I had barely 15 minutes left. Even then there was no time for questions from the audience.

I saw clearly the challenge before me, i.e., not to fall into need, to stay present and not to rush my presentation, to focus on what was really essential. I knew this in my head, but as I began to speak I could feel myself speeding up. My mouth and mind were racing and my body was left far behind. I woke up 15 minutes later, after my mouth, out of sheer exhaustion, had come to a standstill. I was completely disgusted with myself, not because of missing equal time to speak, but because I missed a far more interesting opening.

What I should have done was this. I should have strode into the audience and used the limitation of time as a golden opportunity to focus the audience's attention upon this critical issue in a negotiation: how to turn limitations of time to advantage. I should have asked my listeners what **system** they possessed to seize the initiative in their Japanese or Chinese negotiations when they believed—or were meant to believe—they were out of time (a discovery question). I should have asked each person, as I stood before the conference tables, how he or she stays present when the pressure's on. I should have asked why we westerners feel so compelled to fill things up, to tell instead of ask, to preach instead of learn. And by my questions I would have helped them see, each one, how convention and routine deaden our reflexes into mediocrity. (Each person on the panel, I am sad to say, behaved in this same routinized, competitive way, grasping for attention and positioning for advantage.) I could have done all of this in less than five minutes—there was more than time enough! And then, suddenly, I should have sat down and let the silence settle. In so small a time 200 legal professionals from all over the world would have had a sense of the lightning flash that words can never convey.

Let us turn now to the last of the discovery tools. I refer to PIPs, Player Integrity Profiles.

Brannan: Yes, that's a very interesting subject. Let's deal with that.

Gresser: If character is really the determinant of our destiny, as the Greeks and Chinese have written, what are some of the essential elements by which this source code of action is governed? For if we can uncover the core, we will be able to trace a hundred other qualities that constellate about it. Is there a way to predict how another's foibles from the perspective of integrity will play upon our weaknesses, how another's strengths will enhance our own? How can we use this knowledge for reconnaissance in following the path of The Five Rings?

PLAYER INTEGRITY PROFILES (PIPs)

PIPs (Player Integrity Profiles) affords a first glimpse into character by identifying the most essential elements from the perspective of integrity. The great Chinese military strategist, Sun Tzu, wrote twenty-three hundred years ago, "Know yourself and know your enemy, and you cannot be defeated in a hundred battles. Know yourself but fail to know your enemy, and you will win half the time, and lose the other half. Do not know yourself and fail to know your enemy, and you will lose every battle." PIPs is a modern adaptation of Sun Tzu's basic precept of military strategy.

Here are the essentials of PIPs. See Illustration 4. The first is **the principle of matching/mismatching**. In essence, does the player walk the talk? Does he act as he claims? By observing carefully you will know whether this person is authentic—is someone behind the mask? Or do we have a priest who takes advantage of his flock, a lawyer who bilks his (her) clients, an expert on fitness who smokes or is obese? Whenever you find a mismatch, in a deep sense, you find a flaw in integrity. In PIPs we assess this factor of matching/mismatching, as we do all other elements—low, moderate or high.

The second element is **the principle of containment**. One can think of integrity as a living "container," which is character. By working on character we can build the container. We can learn to "hold integrity" against the assaults of life.

If the container is constricted there is no breath, no life. If the container is too porous, it will hold very little. There can be no integrity. Some people live solitary and shut-up lives, shuttling back and forth like crayfish between dark recesses. Others leak like sieves, pouring out their feelings, needs and opinions to anyone who will listen. Both have serious problems with containment.

PLAYER INTEGRITY PROFILE (PIPS)

Critical Factors	Low	Moderate	High
Matching (No Mismatching)			
Containment			
Trainability			
No Need, Non-Attachment			
The Pain/Need Ratio			
No Assumptions			
No Expectations			
Embraces "No"			
Controls Arrogance, Vanity & Greed			
Sense of Ease/Time to Spare			
Listens			
Ability to Attend			
Focus			
Nurtures			
Gravitas			
Thoroughly Awake & Present			
Sees the World As It Is			
PIPS Total Score			

COMMENT

ILLUSTRATION 4

Trainability is the third element. Does this person embrace error and failure, reach for challenges, adjust nimbly and intelligently? Can she be like water, adapting willingly to the environment? Or is the fear of failure so strong, the self-sabotaging behaviors so entrenched, the character so brittle, that easy change is rarely possible?

No need/no attachment is the fourth element. There is a saying, "The great way is easy. No picking, no choosing." The superior person, the person of integrity, will have few real needs. You will see little clawing for advantage.

The pain/need ratio is the fifth element. Here is an essential clue. How well can this person hold on to integrity before the Face of Pain, or does a little pain bring on a great panic? Persons of high integrity understand how to hold steady (high pain/need ratio) and will find their power within their pain.

No assumptions/no expectations is the sixth. We have already reviewed this principle at length. Find a penchant toward assumption and expectation and you will find a weakness that will breed ten other flaws.

Embraces the 'no' is the seventh. Is this person terrified of 'no,' needs to be right, or unwilling to appear silly or foolish? These qualities flock together.

The eighth element is **arrogance, vanity and greed**. There can be little integrity when these qualities dominate, because everything will be inflated, inverted and distorted.

A sense of ease and time to spare is the ninth test. Those who need to grasp or become servants of their desires and expectations have little time to spare. They will never be at peace.

If they are ill at ease and have no time, how well will they listen, how easily will they attend?

The abilities **to listen well** and **to attend** are the tenth and eleventh elements. They do not always align with a sense of ease and time to spare, but usually they do. It is said, "When the universe roars only the heavenly dragon observes with calm delight." The person of high integrity—the dragon—listens and observes when the rest of the world is steaming.

The twelfth test is **focus**. This quality does not always track with others. A player can have a focus of steel and score poorly in all the other qualities. A person of high integrity, however, who is fully present in the moment, can usually bring extraordinary powers of concentration to any issue at hand.

Nurturing is the next test. When you meet this person do you feel enriched and affirmed in her presence, or does she make you feel more lonely?

Gravitas is the fourteenth variable. *Gravitas* refers to a sense of weightedness—the whole person is before you. Here he is! Right here. Half of him is not musing somewhere in the past, the other half not distracted by the future. Gravitas transforms a person's creative potential into action. Some people have good ideas but can't embody them because they lack *gravitas*. But when you are grounded and connected, you will have the courage to take risks.

Thoroughly awake and present is the fifteenth quality. When you are with this person do you have a sense that someone is at home? I have mentioned Zuigan's test. All of us to one extent or another are living in a dream. The question is how often do we wake up and realize it?

The final test of PIPs is does this person **see the world** objectively, **just as it is**, modestly and without a lot of ego clutter and noise? It is a formidable test because we all view the world in our own unique way, imperfectly.

Brannan: PIPs sounds like a very powerful tool. It would be helpful to give a few examples of its uses.

Gresser: Okay. Suppose you were considering entering into a business partnership with someone. You run a brief character sketch under PIPs based on your observations of how this person conducted himself with you and other people and you come up with the following profile.

- **Matching/mismatching**. Does your prospective partner walk his talk? In some ways well, but in other ways poorly. He says he has a code of action, but often he doesn't follow it.
- **Containment**. He is disciplined about not spilling information, but at the same time he is a terrible braggart and a name-dropper.
- **Pain/need**. He is a trained fighter and holds together well when in pain.
- **No assumptions/no expectations**. Basically, you conclude he is a predator. He has a perverse tendency to assume, then presume upon, and finally to consume others.
- **Embraces the 'no.'** He is focused, disciplined, cunning, and persistent. You find he is quite able to give a 'no,' but you also detect a note of condescension, even irritation in his voice whenever he gets a 'no,' with the suggestion that he believes the other party is an idiot for not agreeing with him.
- **Arrogance, vanity and greed**. He is arrogant and vain, and you discover that behind the mask

there is a consuming piggish appetite for control and power.

- **Focus**. He has advanced powers of concentration and focus, and an almost elephantine memory.
- **Gravitas**. There is no one behind the voice. Deep down you sense he is a shallow, hollow man.

Reflecting upon these qualities, the first question PIPs would naturally urge you to ask yourself is: "Why would you ever want to be in business with such a person?" "Well," you might reply, "he has certain virtues. For example, he is energetic, resourceful and imaginative. He is a street fighter, which complements my own talents and offsets my shortcomings." On an impulse you might want to enter into this partnership, but PIPs would give you pause. If on balance you were to decide to move forward with the partnership despite your reservations, PIPs would focus your attention on other important questions. For example, would this person stand by you during the rough and uncertain times when you might really value a strong partner? Would this person deal with the firm's clients generously or in a grasping manner? And so forth.

PIPs would require you to check yourself: "Given this profile, how might this person play upon—even exploit—my weaknesses?" you might ask yourself. For example, if in drawing your own PIPs profile you conclude you have issues around **gravitas** and **steadiness**, or become particularly disoriented and unfocused around the **pain/need threshold**, you would want to be extremely careful with this person in high-stress situations, and never look to your partner for nourishment or affirmation. Conversely, PIPs would help you better understand how your special strengths— for example, your capacity to listen, presence and trainability—will help you spot the subtle signs and signals of a change of intention that enable you to adjust quickly to his moods as necessary.

By analyzing your opponents and examining yourself with PIPs, you will have a powerful tool to take intelligent action **in advance** in all sorts of other situations as well. PIPs will help you identify precisely the actions and behaviors that are telltale, and those areas of your own vulnerability that require reinforcement. For example, if you know someone to be devious or a bully, who makes you feel inadequate or frightened, (i.e., loss of **gravitas**, **need**, a **sense of helplessness** and **catastrophe**), you can prepare yourself. You can rehearse the script, you can bring someone else along, or you can send a blocker in your place. There are many things you can do to anticipate such situations.

Brannan: It seems to me it is quite difficult to be able to predict accurately our future moods and emotional states which, after all, are sudden and transitory and often bear no direct relationship to the outer world.

Gresser: Yes, I agree. I have noted that things can be going very well in the external world, but then, all of a sudden, we are in a mood, and internally everything is quite dark and melancholy. I would like to return to this subject a bit later when we discuss how to practice.

Brannan: How about situations we don't anticipate?

Gresser: Yes, often these are the most interesting cases, when life suddenly throws us a spinner—for example, a person reveals his or her real character and catches us off guard. PIPs will help us see into the character of such situations and guide our response.

INTEGRITY
CORRUPTED

I remember some years ago I was conducting a training program on negotiation at a large semiconductor company here in California. After the program, the VP for marketing who headed the group thought it would be cute to ignore our bills and not answer our phone calls (see PIPs, principles of **matching/mismatching**; **arrogance**, **vanity**, **greed**; **failure to nurture** or **to see the world as it is**). Amused by this peculiar development, I waited patiently to see what would happen, remembering Emerson's observation, "The thief (under the law of compensation) steals from himself." Sometimes PIPs helps us see that the "right" (simplest and most elegant) move is to do nothing at all. Weeks passed, then months. One day I learned the VP had been fired. He did not attend to the flaws in his character early, and so they surfaced later and in a more corruptive, self-destructive form. I resubmitted my bill to the president of the company and was promptly paid.

Brannan: What about strengths? Can PIPs help guide the choice of a partner so that one person's strengths nourish and reinforce another's?

Gresser: Certainly. The best alliances are symbiotic. I know of several partnerships where one person's modesty, containment and steadiness under pressure have provided *gravitas* to the other whose creative energies, buoyed up by a revived sense of trust, have begun to soar. PIPs has made both parties more conscious of their individual strengths for their mutual advantage.

Brannan: Let us turn now to *lōgōs*, the final essential skill for a player practicing The Five Rings.

Gresser: Okay. But first I'd like to explain a bit about the relationship of *lōgōs* to intuition and reverie.

Brannan: Please do.

Gresser:

When we first came up with lōgōs for the corporate name, we were only generally familiar with its historical significance. To the Greeks, *lōgōs*, or the word (reason), was the ordering principle of the universe, comparable to the Tao for the Chinese. To live in harmony with *lōgōs* was the goal of all seekers of wisdom. Later in the Gospel of John, *lōgōs* is transformed into the divine word that exists with God and is uniquely embodied in Jesus Christ.

We define *lōgōs* more simply. It is logic, common sense, and intelligence, combined with intuition in action. Thus defined, *lōgōs* is virtually identical with the Chinese conception of integrity (*te*).

Brannan:

How is *lōgōs* used in practice?

Gresser:

I'll tell you a story of how I once used *lōgōs* in reconnaissance, and after that give one example of how *lōgōs* can help us identify the next best move.

Three years ago I had a legal client who was a very rich man, a visionary, and also a small-time tycoon. He had an ambitious project to develop the San Francisco Bay. How he promised me the world! Opera tickets appeared in the mail, and there were invitations to exclusive dinner parties.

Common sense should have told me to be circumspect, to investigate, to get a better hold on this man and his promises. But I was so enchanted with what he told me—his vision had become my vision—that I didn't pay much attention to what logic urged or my common sense advised.

Somewhere along the way I began to feel uneasy, and I decided to ask my integrity. I should elaborate on this phrase, "ask my integrity," since it involves a bit of technique. The first thing I did was to get fully present within myself. I relaxed, let go, became conscious of the ebb and flow of my breath tides. I allowed whatever thoughts or feelings or images waited below the surface of consciousness to approach. When I began to experience a floating feeling—as if I were just watching a play from the balcony (this state of consciousness is called "creative reverie")—I said to myself, "What should I know about this person that I may be overlooking?"

Minutes passed, and I continued to relax, just to let go. I was in the zone of nothing special. Suddenly an image appeared, as if from nowhere. A mouth! A fine mouth it was, possessed of white, polished teeth.

"This is rather peculiar," I thought. (I was now leaving reverie.) "What is a mouth with white polished teeth?" So I began to examine the image more closely.

I began with the mouth. It was a large, gaping mouth. A mouth, it occurred to me, is the beginning of the digestive process—something like the First Circle in Dante's *Inferno*. Then I said to myself, "What are teeth?" Well, teeth are the tools of the digestive process, by which we chew up food. I was beginning to have an unsettled feeling in my stomach, but I proceeded.

"What is white?" I asked myself. "Dignified, polished, sophisticated— how interesting!"

So I bundled these associations together and then I said to myself, "My Lord, what can all this mean? What conceivable link can there be to my original question?" And then suddenly, from nowhere, the idea came to me. "The Man is a Polished Carnivore!!" A polished carnivore? Can this be? Let me investigate.

Remember, we do not assume, we only observe when

something singular comes up. So that's what I did. I started to pay more attention to his moods and to our interactions, and soon I began to notice all sorts of things that probably were there all along, but I did not see them before—implicitly obvious, I would say—little (in)significant things: the intrusive phone calls, the demands that I put aside important work to accommodate **his** schedule—like the time he showed up and snatched a half-completed letter out of my secretary's typewriter. Soon I saw a different face behind the mask—an arrogant, grinning, entitled face of a person who, on a whim, would toss aside his promises, dishonor a bill, or betray me. I knew this part of him perhaps better than he knew it himself. And so two to three weeks before he suspended the project and began to quibble about his bill, I was prepared, and so was my firm.

Brannan: Interesting. What lessons do you draw from this case?

Gresser: The key lesson is that we have enormous untapped capabilities and powers that we do not know how to use; and that by a disciplined procedure we can bring logic, common sense and intelligence to bear on important issues, and join these with our intuitive powers when taking practical action. Our integrity is what opens the channel, the connection between conscious and unconscious processes. We receive continuous information and advice from sources that are a part of us, but of which we have only been vaguely aware. In this case, it was the image of a mouth. Each situation calls forth its own imagery. But we do not follow these instructions blindly. We return to our intelligence and common sense, always testing, observing like a scientist. And when our intellect does not give us a completely satisfactory answer, we feel our way through. We listen to our bodies and ask, "Does this seem right or not?" and our body will answer.

Brannan: How does this process apply to identifying the "best next move"?

Gresser: Let us return to The Five Rings. To find the best next move all you need to do in any encounter is follow this simple procedure. First examine how well you have performed each of the moves in the circle in which you now stand. Have you jumped the sequence of rings or jumped a move? What errors have you committed? If you conclude you have done reasonably well, ask yourself this question: "How can I do even better next time?" This is the analytic function.

                If you have played well, celebrate your wins and remember to take the joy and the benefits and to pass them onward, selflessly, without thought of recognition or recompense. This is called "paying forward." It is the most powerful technique I know to dispel feelings of helplessness and despair and to enhance self-image, clarity and power.

                After you have centered yourself in this way, to find the best next move, you need only ask yourself this next question: "Given what I have learned in this situation, what move will best advance my mission and build integrity?" If your analytic mind blocks you, you may decide to bypass it by checking into reverie and repeating the question. An answer, or many answers, will appear if you are patient. They must appear, because you are reconnected, and every answer so conceived will be the "right" one.

Brannan: You know, this issue of "best moves" raises for me a final and perhaps odd question. Suppose your opponents read this book and use the same principles against you and your clients? As a professional person, aren't you a bit concerned about giving your secrets away?

Gresser: It's in my interest that they learn these secrets. What do you mean "against"? In this situation there's no "against"! How am I diminished if my opponents become more effective by enhancing their integrity?—if they become clearer about what they want, build missions of service, are not attached or needy, exercise self-control, focus on my pain, and are at ease and adaptable to change? Their "best" move will most likely turn out to be quite "good" for me. If even one player plays this game, you start to enter a realm of magic. Look at the Getz case. With only one set of the parties (ourselves) consciously playing in this way, we produced a landmark result extraordinarily profitable for everyone—the owners, the investing public, the managers, the employees, underwriters, even the Japanese and U.S. governments. We never gave a thought once to trying to reach a "win-win" result. And that was very early in the development of my thinking about these matters. Can you imagine if everyone starts to play the game this way?! Then you will see lightning decisions springing from foresight and wisdom; good humor and sport and surprise everywhere; some sparks, to be sure, but little clawing for personal aggrandizement or advantage, for it will be a roughhouse and creative combat of dragons!

IV. How to Practice

Where shall I take the hit?
What must be sacrificed
and to which gods?
— The Artful Navigator

Just do the important thing that is right before you.
— The Artful Navigator

Too broad? Narrow it. Too vague? Clarify it. Too general? Be more specific.
Too abstract? Be more concrete. Too dense? Simplify it. If lost in the forest,
move toward the sky. If too near the sun, reduce elevation, return to
the earth.
— The Artful Navigator

Modesty. Do simple work. Some of the great martial artists were clerks in
a hotel. We do our work in the world without much interest in glory.
Our ideal is to live inconspicuously in the town among the people.
— The Artful Navigator

Take the world lightly, and your spirit will not be burdened. Consider
everything minor and your mind will not be confused. Regard death
and life as equal and your heart will not be afraid.
— Masters of Huainan

IV. How to Practice

Brannan: Julian, you have explained the theoretical foundation for our work, and have outlined the framework of play, The Five Rings, and the core skills. But, as we all know, someone can read a book, listen to a tape, go to a seminar, gain a conceptual understanding, and not be able to do very much of anything. The gap between theory and practice is too great. The key is training. What are some of your recommendations as to how a person who is interested in dedicating him or herself to this material can go about attaining real skill?

Gresser: A great Chinese general, Wang Yang Ming, whose profession compelled him to be practical, once observed, "Knowledge without action is not knowledge at all." We study this material by doing it. There are no shortcuts. And the key to mastery is what the Japanese call *kaizen*—continuous improvement at the margin. The Five Ring system is the *kaizen* of action.

Brannan: What is the first step?

Gresser: Tracking. Tracking is the first step. To be a great negotiator one must become a great observer and like Cassius see quite through the deeds of men. We can make a science of our daily life. Watch. Here's how.

The first thing I recommend is to keep a Weekly Log. See Illustration 5. In form the log is simple. In my design, at the top is the overall weekly mission. Below are the four quadrants of life: professional, personal, physical and spiritual. Underneath is space to record discoveries relating to the overall weekly mission or to more specific goals in each quadrant. There is also space to enter insights and discoveries relating to the missions or, more generally, discoveries that simply

THE WEEKLY LOG

THE WEEKLY LOG

MISSION:

DATE:

Professional	Spiritual	Physical	Personal

Weekly Practice Move/Principle

Discoveries (M&P)	Pay Forward

Discovery, Joy, Wonder and Magic

ILLUSTRATION 5

open us to joy, wonder and magic. The box on the right provides space to enter instances of paying forward.

Brannan: Why did you choose a week instead of a day or a month?

Gresser: Let me make clear the purposes of the Weekly Log. The first purpose is to restore coherence. We live lives divided from ourselves. Most people's professional lives are divorced from their spiritual aspirations. Their work pulls against—if not tears apart—their family life. Their physical mission, if there is any, is an afterthought. The first purpose, then, of the Weekly Log is to restore integrity.

The second purpose of the Weekly Log is discovery. I have found that every move, every step in a negotiation is a point of discovery—about ourselves and the other players. I have also found there are patterns in the stream of discoveries and images in our life, and this stream runs just below the surface of consciousness, implicit yet obvious, when you train the eye to see it. The Weekly Log is designed as a camera to open the eye and to take snapshots of these discoveries.

A third objective is to focus the powers of concentration on a single weakness or strength. We can make far greater progress if we pick one skill or one principle of behavior and concentrate all our energies there, for a space of time, rather than hop like a bird each day to a different flower.

To achieve these three purposes, the Weekly Log is optimal—a day is far too short, a month impractically long. After all, who has the patience to concentrate on one thing for a month?

Brannan: I would like to get quickly into the substance of how one actually practices with a Weekly Log, but I can't help anticipating that the idea of writing down your "magic" in a box on a Weekly Log may simply send shivers up the spine of some artistic and creative people. Aren't you tampering here with something almost sacred?

Gresser:
You raise, you realize, the magician's dilemma. There are many conjurers in this world—some of surpassing talent—who can draw out of the mists the most fantastic forms. But can they finish the task? Do they know how to let go, to launch their creation? When air, water, fire and earth meet that is where you must take your stand. Here is where magicians, conjurers and tricksters run aground and often are consumed by their own powers. Great courage and fortitude—integrity—is demanded at this point to resist being pushed around by the elements and to take the action of bringing your creation into the world.

It is the common illusion of some people that order and creativity are incompatible. I know a wonderful woman, a philanthropist, who has supported many worthy causes. Some weeks ago, as we discussed my methods over lunch, she said to me with a wave of her hand, "I don't believe in logic." Can you imagine? Creativity for her is pure mystery that simply flies in through the window.

And yet, when you study the lives of the great creative geniuses—Michelangelo, Picasso, Mozart, Bach, Beethoven, Dickens—and not only men and women artists, writers and composers, but also scientists and discoverers—you will find that most of them had an explicit method—no, I will go further—they all had a **system**. This is the point Peter Ackroyd makes in his monumental study of Dickens, and it is echoed in Arthur Koestler's classic study of creativity, and by researchers such as Robert Root-Bernstein and

Howard Gardner. In my experience the critical guideline in working with the creative forces—and I agree with you that we **are** working with something most sacred—is profound respect. We can set the boundary conditions through a method—prepare the compost and plant the seeds, so to speak—but then we must step back, leave room, and be careful not to bear down too much. If you treat the Muse as you would your dearest friend, my experience suggests you will be on the right track to knowing each other in a free and exploratory way.

Brannan: It seems there is much art in linking the processes of creativity and effective action. But we should move on. Let's return to basics. How does one actually practice with the Weekly Log?

Gresser: After getting clear about your mission, the Weekly Log helps you focus on the cases that challenge your skill in each quadrant—a formal negotiation, a meeting, a phone call, even a chance encounter are all "cases." Through these cases the game is played, the battle is won or lost.

Brannan: What is the next step?

Gresser: After organizing my practice in the Weekly Log, I chart the "wave form" of a day. I have discovered that each day has its special pattern, and, more interestingly, as we begin to understand and to settle into its ebb and flow, we can influence in a modest way the course of events we generally assume to be quite outside our control.

Brannan: How do you mean?

Gresser: Let me first describe the content of the Charts and then mention a few interesting discoveries I have made along the way.

I track fourteen indices, many of which may now be familiar. On the top line I trace the flow of "external" events by the hour. Above the line is "positive," meaning something "good" has happened; below it, something unpleasant or negative has occurred. Here and elsewhere I chart ideas, occurrences and happenings that seem to me significant. The external line is the external wave form of my life for this day. The remaining fourteen lines trace developments in the "inner" world. I am interested in the interplay of the inner with the outer.

The second line is the line of **Emotions**. Above are the emotions reflecting joy, excitement, triumph and inflation. Below are fears, doubts, negative humors or moods. Sometimes the emotions are tranquil, but at other times they become turbulent, either by becoming inflated or depressed.

Need is the third line, the **Sense of Ease and Time to Spare** is the fourth, a **Sense of Catastrophe** the fifth. I have observed a recursive pattern between them. As **Need** goes up, the **Sense of Ease and Time to Spare** drops off. When need persists, catastrophe appears. None of this, of course, may have any relationship to what is actually happening in the "external" realm. Thus we believe a catastrophe is upon us, when often it is only a phantom, a figment of our emotions and imagination.

Vanity, Arrogance and Grandiosity occupy the next line. I have already mentioned the perverse relationship that is possible with these qualities. I know some people who when they get vain, grandiose or inflated, instantly get swatted. Actually, it may be a sign that they are progressing in the practice of integrity. I came upon this discovery working through the Charts.

Brannan: Can you give an example?

Gresser: All right. When my creative juices are really flowing, or I have achieved a major breakthrough in a negotiation, that moment is when I am most vulnerable. If for a second I start feeling that I am superior, brighter or more entitled, at that very moment, or perhaps even before I become aware, my creativity will start to flag, or I will be out of sync with the move of my opponent, or I will miss an important opportunity. I have created a "distance," stopped listening, and fallen out of touch. I'm sure athletes encounter this same phenomenon on the tennis court or the baseball and football fields. I meet it in the arena of negotiation.

Brannan: What comes next?

Gresser: The **Ability to Manage the Trolls**.

Brannan: The who?

Gresser: (Laughs) The Trolls. Trolls, as you may know, are swart, smelly creatures who live under bridges (often spiritual bridges). Although they seem the stuff of fairy tales, actually Trolls can take "real" form in moods or humors. They are the melancholy voices that say to us, "Why try to accomplish that or really anything at all? You're not up to that. Why even try. You're over the hill." Professor Michael Ray of the Stanford Business School refers to these unpleasant creatures as the Voice of Judgment. There is also an excellent book on the subject by Richard Carson called *Taming Your Gremlin*. A sense of humor is one of the keys to dealing with the Trolls. Your ability to laugh at yourself and to be present when they're around sends the Trolls squealing away much like garlic routed the Devil during the Middle Ages.

ABILITY TO
MANAGE THE
TROLLS

Seeing the World as it Really Is is the next element. As need drops and the emotions settle down, the world becomes clearer, friendlier and more simple.

The Will (or Volition) to Combat Helplessness is the next. Particularly in these times of turbulence and uncertainty, when almost everyone feels alone and powerless, the Will to combat helplessness can be a guide through the darkest days.

The Ability to Attend, *Gravitas,* **Steadiness and Trust in the Connection** are the next set of variables. When you work on steadiness and *gravitas* you begin to trust in your native capabilities, and then you regain hope and come out to see the world.

Life Force or Vitality (meaning physical, mental and spiritual energy) is the next element. The Chinese call it *chi,* the Japanese *ki,* and the Indians *prana.* You can feel when the *chi* is flowing and then you know you are in the integrity state.

Pay Forward is the next variable. When need and arrogance are down and my life force is engaged, I feel abundant. Giving freely without any thought of recompense, I express my power.

Discovery, Joy, Wonder and Magic is the next variable. When you feel vital and you sense the connection to the world around you, the connection becomes palpable. It is reinforced in every moment. You don't have to do anything. You can feel it in your bones. Just let your eyes be dazzled.

Sense of Effectiveness. This is the last element. No matter how wild the weather is, I can keep my hands firmly upon the wheel. I have seen such seas and I have made it through before.

Brannan: And what have you discovered in your tracking?

Gresser: I have discovered that the outer and the inner are independent, and yet connected intimately. Things can be proceeding magnificently in our outer life, while all of a sudden a mood takes over and we are out of sorts. Although this insight may seem commonplace enough, it is of vital importance to negotiators, because it refocuses us on objective reality: things may seem topsy-turvy, but are they really? How truly insignificant are many of the cares that now seem so important to us? Like the wind, most of them are passing vanities, signifying nothing.

The second insight for me is more remarkable. I have found that by restoring "integrity" in the inner, it is possible to influence the outer.

Brannan: Let's take this more slowly. I'm not sure I follow what you're saying.

Gresser: Look, every good sports psychologist or martial artist understands that by developing certain psycho-physiological powers we can affect external events. The movie, *Chariots of Fire*, is a good example. Coach Mastrobini worked not only on Harold Abrahms' physical body so that he could endure the rigors of the race, but equally importantly, the Coach worked on his character, and as a result Harold Abrahms became an Olympic champion and years later the Elder Statesman of British sports.

I have discovered that when things "go south" on the external line, by restoring integrity on any line in the inner, the "system" somehow recalibrates, and then the external becomes positive too.

Brannan: How does it become positive?

Gresser: In many ways. We can get a phone call from an old friend whom we have not seen in many years. A conflict gets resolved. A contract we have been seeking comes through. Someone dear to us has a great success. The universe seems to be laughing. "I see you!" it says, "But don't take any of this too seriously." And so we don't.

Brannan: How do you mean, "any line"?

Gresser: Any move that restores integrity—for example, exercising the **Will to combat helplessness**, becoming less **arrogant**, **paying forward**, or simply **attending**, appears to be sufficient to begin to turn the Wheel a degree or so, and that shifts the field. This seems to me to be of enormous significance in these chaotic times, because it says we have more dominion over our life than we ever supposed possible. We have the power to change course instantly whenever we will it, and we can begin right now with little things. It is a discovery that brings hope.

Brannan: It might be helpful to demonstrate this relationship between inner and outer psychic processes with one of your charts.

Gresser: Okay. Here is an illustration of what I call the "wave form" of a day. Now please understand I make no claim to scientific exactitude, only that I and others with whom I have worked have found it helpful to trace the daily patterns in the ebb and flow of integrity.

The first thing to notice on the chart (See Illustration 6 on page 122-123) is that this day started off as many days, with "nothing special." The player attempted four phone calls and was unable to make contact. The external line is flat.

Coincidentally, however, there is already movement

in the inner realm. The **emotions** are starting to plummet. Melancholy and a depression are coming on. **Need** is on the rise. The **sense of ease** and **time to spare** is off kilter. **Catastrophe** is brewing. The **ability to manage the trolls** is in disarray. The player has momentarily forgotten everything he or she once knew about troll management. The **vital life force** is draining out and the player's **capacity to see the world objectively** is, like Humpty Dumpty, sitting on its head. And for what justifiable reason? No reason.

Next. Around 9:00 a.m. the player says to him or herself, "Enough! I'm not going along with this travesty." Here is the Exercise of Choice — the Act of Will! Now watch. A new inner process begins to stir. The **ability to attend**, **gravitas** and **steadiness** regroups. Once again the player is beginning to **trust in the connection**. His/her **life force** also revives. **Vanity, arrogance and grandiosity** (for many of our daily terrors are really just forms of vanity and grandiosity) begin to subside. The **sense of effectiveness**, this player's capacity to grapple, is also strengthening.

Things get even more interesting between 10:00 a.m. and 12:00 p.m. On the external line the player starts to receive some positive feedback. A key business contact he/she has been trying to reach is at home and the conversation produces a good result. Next, a former client offers to provide invaluable assistance on an ambitious project. Then the player's partner enthusiastically supports a new strategy. You see the mists are lifting. The player is starting to enjoy this mysterious process.

One hour follows the next along this general pattern. A little falling off occurs toward the late afternoon as the player's energy flags. Perhaps some overconfident coasting has set in. And then upon returning home after a pleasant meeting with a colleague, a sur-

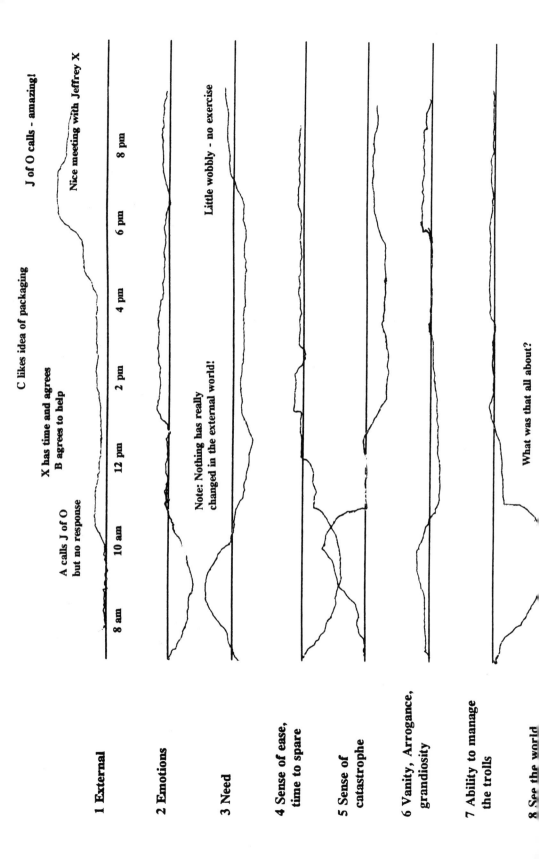

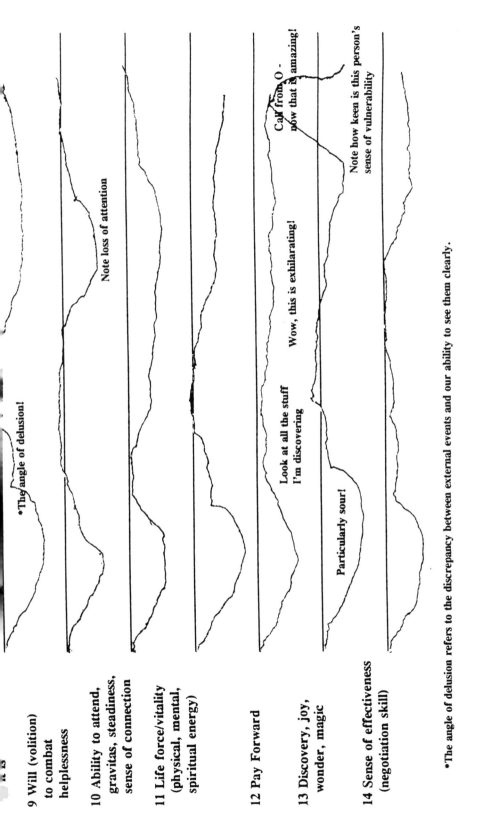

9 Will (volition)
to combat
helplessness

*The angle of delusion!

10 Ability to attend,
gravitas, steadiness,
sense of connection

Note loss of attention

11 Life force/vitality
(physical, mental,
spiritual energy)

12 Pay Forward

Look at all the stuff
I'm discovering

Wow, this is exhilarating!

Particularly sour!

Call from O -
now that is amazing!

13 Discovery, joy,
wonder, magic

14 Sense of effectiveness
(negotiation skill)

Note how keen is this person's
sense of vulnerability

*The angle of delusion refers to the discrepancy between external events and our ability to see them clearly.

ILLUSTRATION 6

prise is waiting: a message from a prospect over a project the player has given up and long forgotten. "We want to do the deal! Can you help us?" the message says. "How can this be? It is so wildly unanticipated," the player asks him or herself.

What conclusions can we draw from this example?

First and most basic, we can play at any point upon the Wheel, and that will be precisely the perfect point! The gate is always open, especially when things are murky and look impossible. That's exactly when you're close—when things are most intimate and you can look inside them. Because each thing, each situation is essentially non-linear yet continuous, and that's what makes it so interesting.

The second point reinforces the first: The downturns, the dark places in our life, they also have a structure. Winter, too, is an orderly process.

The chart implies the third point. If you were to follow the patterns over days and weeks, I believe you might discover, as I have now done for several years, that the process proceeds in spirals. The basic issues of dark and light roll up, day by day, except that the waves are different and so are the faces.

There is no need to be a passive actor in this process. I have found that when we "hold integrity" as this person has done as the waves crest and crash about us, the next round in the cycle becomes richer and even more vibrant and friendly. It takes time but the opening will be there if you can stay conscious enough to embrace it.

To put the same point slightly differently, what I am saying is that there is a fertility in weakness, that the dark times ground and set off the light, and that the

pain we all have to one degree or another has a wonderful energy when we know how to harvest it.

The charts are like a mirror. They are one point of
reference. We can use them to learn to love our life
a little better—as Rilke writes, "to learn to love the
questions" without our overly identifying with them.

Brannan:	You mentioned one other discovery.
Gresser:	I have found it is possible to "change" the past, if by the "past" we mean our memories and our interpretation of it. And if this is so, we can also rewrite the future which is colored and shaped by the past.

Tracking our progress and our mistakes in the Weekly
Log and the Charts, we continue to train over the
weeks and months. Gradually our integrity deepens.
As I have suggested, integrity involves a certain plas-
ticity or trainability of spirit. One of the great attrib-
utes of this spirit is the ability to look around corners,
to see the light side of dark things, and the shadow
in the good. With this eye we can go back and trace
the history of things that have been. And what do we
find? We find, from the advantage of a developed
integrity, that events that once appeared perverse
(below the external line) may have seeded many good
things. We give thanks to these reverses of fortune,
because if they had not happened we could not have
become what we are.

Brannan:	Charting the wave form of one's life seems a fasci- nating exercise but what is the essential benefit from the point of view of the practice?
Gresser:	If the Weekly Log builds integrity in the four quad- rants of life, the Charts help us see what wondrous things can happen when the inner and outer selves become as one. If the secret to piloting through chaos

is presence—when we can be belly-to-belly with our darkest terrors, and they give way to light—then the ability to trace the process, to bring it back before our face, so that we can say, upon reflection, "Yes, this has really happened!" may be the essential tool in our entire arsenal.

Let us move on to one last way to measure the process. I refer to the Action Log.

Brannan: The Action Log has served me well.

Gresser: Like the Weekly Log, the Action Log (see Illustration 7) serves several functions. Each Action Log contains ten decisions which comprise the essentials of the Five Rings system. These decisions address: What we want, our mission, actions and behaviors, the decision makers and their process, pain, budget, agenda, our presentation, discoveries, wins and losses, and finally pay forward. (Please note: The key actions and behaviors in the Action Log are separately listed and do not have to be "in step" with each other.) The Action Log records not only where we "stand" in each negotiation, it also helps us focus. In using the Action Log I recommend picking one principle or move at a time in tracking performance in a specific encounter.

THE ACTION LOG

I find it useful for a player each week to track 5 times he or she practices a particular principle or move, and what are the results; then 5 times in a similar situation the player doesn't bother to practice and the results. And finally, 5 times the player neglects to practice, but then catches the error midstream, adjusts, and consciously deploys the move or principle, and the results. Although there is nothing absolute about "5," it offers a useful way to provide an initial meaningful sampling.

A final use of the Action Log is to seize the initiative.

ACTION LOG

Name of Other Player(s)   Date

Decision   1.   What do I really want?   _____
Decision   2.   Determine the path of action (mission)   _____
Decision   3.   Set Goals for:

Action(s)   **Behavior** (No need)

1. Discovery questions   1. Relax
   a.
   b.   2. Listen and Observe w/Empty Mind
   c.   a. Am I thoroughly awake and present?
2. Check point   3. No Assumptions/Expectations
3. Take notes   4. Nurture (do not fear the 'no')
4. Investigate assumption   5. Focus
5. 'No'   6. Use Your Pain to Find Your Power
   a. Recognize other players' <u>right</u> to say 'no'
   b. Exercise your right of 'no'
   6. Assess your own budget (time x energy x money x emotion)
   7. Cultivate the Will

OTHER PLAYERS

Decision   4.   Determine the other player's principal pain(s)

Decision   5.   Determine the other player's budget   _____
                  (Time x energy x money x emotion)

Decision   6.   Uncover the real decision makers
                  and their process   _____
                                           _____

Decision   7.   Set a valid agenda:

   a. Problems _____   d. What I want _____

      _____

   b. My concerns _____   e. What happens next _____

   c. Other player's concerns _____

Decision   8.   Did I present my case only after making Decisions 1 through 8?   Yes/No
                  a. If no, how leaky was I?

===

Decision 9. Analyze Your Wins,   Decision 10. Pay the Benefits Forward
            Errors & Discoveries

ILLUSTRATION 7

As I have mentioned, every negotiation affords an opening. I play, you respond—it really doesn't matter what you do—if I have integrity, I will hold the "initiative" in the counter play. This is why the analysis of wins and errors in Decision 9 is so essential. The Action Log is a tool to help us find the "winning" counter move.

Brannan: Julian, I would like to raise a practical concern now that you have explained all the ways of tracking and measuring the process. I believe many people will find much merit in the overall spirit of your approach and in some of the techniques. But who has the time to practice in this way? Most people have families to take care of or pressing business priorities. Do you really believe they will make room in their lives to dedicate themselves seriously to the extent your system seems to require?

Gresser: This of course is a critical question, and here is the best way I can respond to it. The method does require an investment of time and effort and creative energy, especially in the beginning. Like the martial arts or any sport, or really any enterprise in life of value, one cannot become an expert in a day. Steady practice is essential. The good news here, however, is there is immediate reinforcement. This is important because no one need take anything on faith. You can instantly derive benefit from practicing any of the principles and moves, and by paying attention to the results. Tracking the process is actually less time-consuming than might first appear. Preparing a Weekly Log or the Charts takes only 15-20 minutes. Each Action Log is about the same. If time is limited I recommend focusing the Action Log on important negotiations, and using the Charts when things really become turbulent. There is also a natural learning curve which has this curious side effect: the entire process tends to become second nature and internalized. Without taking the time physically to prepare an Action Log, you naturally begin to think and act with greater clarity or in terms of missions of service, staying present, looking for the pain points, holding together, paying forward, and enjoying the play of inner and outer processes. Personally I have found the Weekly Log, the Action Log and the Charts continuously useful, but also I have a curiosity about prowling around in such things. A final key point: it's not the length of time you practice that matters, but rather the seriousness of the practice. As you progress you can accomplish in 15 minutes what might have taken you two to three hours several years before, and with a greater sense of ease and play.

Brannan: I think it would be useful at this point to summarize the essentials of the practice.

Gresser: I agree. They are:

- Practice at first in low-risk situations. Enjoy the process of tumbling.
- Keep a record of your "wins" and "losses." Explore their causes.
- Study how to seize the initiative by the re-reaction.
- Pick one behavioral quality, one move or principle each week and concentrate your efforts here, on this single element.
- Become curious about the "hits," pay forward the gains.
- A few mottoes:
  - Integrity is built through modest and simple acts.
  - Every moment, every situation presents an opportunity for training.
  - Continuity is power.
- Be serious and practice hard; do fewer things but do them more deeply; penetrate and taste the authentic flavor.

- Practice everything with everything. In an integrity system **every** move you make connects to every other, so that any incremental improvement in one immediately and at the margin enhances the integrity of all.

In my own practice, I have trained myself each night to review before my mind's eye these five questions:

- What are the points of beauty of this day? We so easily pass them by and then we forget. I find that it is in beauty that we can revitalize and recreate ourselves.
- How shall I express them?
- What have I discovered?
- By what case?
- How can I embody this discovery more fully?

To me the truly wonderful things in life—how we meet our loved one, for example—come like a summer's day without our bidding and seem to bear no relationship to anything we have done before. And yet we can create the conditions by modest, steady attention each day to our integrity: paying attention to what we have learned from the drama, polishing, polishing, polishing . . . . If we can do this, only this, I have found that even the most mundane tasks or encounters become interesting and meaningful and will reveal, if we are disposed to look, surprises and their special touch of magic.

V. The Lōgōs Network

Glendower: *"I can call spirits from the vasty deep."*

Hotspur: *"Why so can I, or so can any
man; but will they come when you do
call for them?"*
       — Shakespeare - Henry IV, Part I

*"Fantasies these will seem, to such as are able to call my
beginning an ordinary effort."*
       — T.E. Lawrence

V. The Lōgōs Network

Brannan:
We have come very far. It may be useful in this last section for our students and others to have a sense of our personal vision, of the path that lies before us.

Gresser:
Let us summarize where we are. We began with the predicament of many people today who feel that the ground under their lives is beginning to shake. The thread that can lead us through the labyrinth is integrity, and integrity is a trainable skill. The path must be one of service, which is called the mission. The process of carrying out the mission, i.e., the negotiation, never ends, and the secret to holding steady and moving through chaos is to come to grips with the universality of pain. For when we can stay present to our pain and the pain of others the process of navigation becomes the vehicle of our transformation.

Brannan:
It seems you are extending the concept of "path of service," "pain" and "transformation" primarily to business settings which really are a far cry from the true sacrifices and real suffering these terms carry for many people. For me, "path of service" suggests people like Mother Teresa or Albert Schweitzer who at great personal risk have selflessly given of themselves, and through that process have discovered a deeper reverence, satisfaction and fulfillment in life. Is it really appropriate to use these same words to refer to cases like Getz or Flanagan, which involve people who simply acted intelligently in challenging business situations and were well remunerated?

Gresser:
I do not mean to dishonor or in any way to trivialize by some of the business examples I have used the profound contribution of people like Mother Teresa or Albert Schweitzer. They and many others less celebrated are extraordinary people who have done

extraordinary things, and their work can be an inspiration to us. But not everyone can be Mother Teresa or Albert Schweitzer or feel their special kind of calling. And yet I believe there are many people who hope to find in their work a way to be of some use and help to others. Of course, businesses solve this problem by giving to charities, and many people do community service on the side. What I am saying, which may be radical, is that it is not necessary to split off what you do to earn a living from the deeper sense of satisfaction and fulfillment I am speaking of. Everyone has some level of loneliness and pain. The cultivation of integrity, whether through the mission, the practice of presence, paying forward or whatever, is a way to connect to and allay that loneliness and pain, and in that process we can find new meaning, satisfaction and refreshment in work. If good works were limited to the Mother Teresas of the world, I fear we would be in a sorry state since there are so few of them. But who's to say what will be the cumulative positive effects of thousands of chance interactions among people who might start to act and think in this way? I believe we must extend the concept of service to the daily activities of people if we are to cope with the changes fast coming on us.

Brannan: What kinds of changes?

Gresser: I see rough weather ahead. One doesn't require a special gift of prophesy to foresee increasing misery as more and more people around the world go hungry, as the living environment is destroyed, as ancient and new diseases run rampant, as militant fundamentalism, bigotry and violence snuff out those who call for temperance, beauty and reason.

Brannan: And yet so many people appear to be indifferent to all of this—they are too busy, too preoccupied.

Gresser: There is too much suffering in the world to be pre-occupied, to live superficially. Although the problems at times seem overwhelming, I believe there is a practical basis for hope.

With regard to the vision of our enterprise and the path before us, there are three premises on which we might productively begin:

- First, a serious and concerted effort to restore integrity is necessary individually, within organizations and communities, at the national level and among nations. Integrity has been much impaired.
- Second, technology can make a constructive contribution in the development and diffusion of the essential skills.
- Third, the problems before us are so over-whelming—we are too interconnected—for each of us to solve them alone. We must invent new ways of helping each other move through.

Brannan: You and I place great store in technology. I wonder if we are overstressing its role?

Gresser: We live in an Age of Information, of Digital Super-Highways and Virtual Cyberspace. But are these things bringing us greater comfort, well-being or happiness? I think not. In many ways the tools we are producing are producing more noise, more confusion, more alienation and fragmentation. Are we any wiser because we have computers and our electronic networks?

I agree with you that the tools are not the answer. People, not technology, will bring about the beneficial changes I foresee. But the tools can help.

Brannan: How would you like to proceed?

Gresser: I would like to begin with a classical model which is
                curiously pertinent to the problems of this troubled
                age.

Brannan: Fine.

Gresser: Long ago, it is said, in ancient China people lived
                close to the earth (the *Tao*) and tilled the soil in both
                its physical and metaphysical sense (meaning char-
                acter or integrity). In each village you could hear the
                dogs barking and the cocks crowing, but no one
                intruded on his neighbor. Formal rules and moral-
                ity had little use in this society, because people lived
                in a natural way in harmony with themselves and each
                other. The leader was a balanced and complete
                person (in Chinese, chuan·tz), one who was skilled
                both in the martial and the peace-loving arts. He or
                she (for the Taoists did not discriminate against
                women) ruled by example, not by cold command or
                punishments.

                Of what relevance is the Taoist model to these con-
                fused times? I believe in many ways. It is modest and
                frugal, which has appeal in this era of privitization
                and fiscal conservatism. It is skeptical of avarice or
                incompetence, especially in leaders. Thus it returns
                political power to the town and village. It respects the
                voices of local communities everywhere to express
                themselves. It honors character. And at its core are
                timeless human values such as the solidity of the fam-
                ily—of such political concern today—that uphold
                integrity and reaffirm life.

                I believe we can engraft this classical model right on
                the limbs of modern society and the medium will be
                an imaginative use of technology.

Brannan: How in the most practical ways do you believe com-
                puter technology can help this metamorphosis?

Gresser: I would like to discuss how computers can help people acquire the skills of integrity by serving as a virtual executive coach.

This is particularly useful in solving the problem of "fall-off" which plagues everyone who goes through a workshop or seminar. How much do most people really remember two or three weeks after a workshop? Very little. How many participants can really put into practice what they have learned? Few indeed. These are skills—true life skills—that depend as much upon the hand as upon the head. Development of integrity is like the martial arts. You cannot obtain a black belt in a weekend. Continuous practice **in system** supported by coaching is key.

There are three areas where computer technology can help us overcome the limitations of our own physical and mental faculties. The first and most obvious is memory. In training it is invaluable, as I have said, to track and to review our discoveries so that the new skills, the new learning, is assimilated. But who has the memory to keep on top of all of this? If you ask anyone, "On this very day three months ago, what was your most important discovery?" few people would have an answer. And yet if you were to ask the average thinking person, "How unimportant are your discoveries?" she would protest and tell you, "Why, they are the stepping stones that give meaning to my life!" Why then do we squander what is most precious?

If the computer, this electro-mechanical apparatus, has any virtue, it has memory. Perhaps then it can serve as a modern, less poetic version of Mnemosyne (Memory), who in Greek mythology was the mother of the Muses. Computers can help us recall all the points of beauty and discovery that have been put away and long forgotten but which are embedded in their electronic minds. They give us a second chance to relive these memories.

There is another significant use of computers not generally observed. Coping with the challenges of this age demands every bit of our ingenuity and creative vitality. Since these resources are not inexhaustible, the question is how can we conserve and deploy them most efficiently? The first issue is how do we account? In business today many people have time or money management systems. But how many have a means to keep track of effort, or even more importantly, can account for their "expenditures" of creativity? No one I know in business, much less in family life, "accounts" for expenditures of creativity. And yet by ignoring this most precious of all resources we unconsciously assign a value to creativity and that value is 0. It is startling to consider that almost everyone in business today is misallocating resources by not "pricing" expenditures of creativity. In less taxing times such laxity can pass unnoticed. Not in these times.

We have developed a simple and reliable way to use the computer in measuring and recording expenditures of time, effort, financial reserves and creative emotion (vitality) in the form of integrity budget units (IBUs). When first organizing the life mission a player sets the IBUs in the life pie and then inputs expenditures in cases under The Five Rings. With one click a player or a team can instantly bring up on the screen a bar graph of the original budget and the amount of IBUs consumed as of that date. By tracking expenditures in any project or case the computer helps to prevent waste and to use our "gifts" more efficiently.

Brannan: I hope you do not expect, Julian, that economists are going to flock to us with open arms.

Gresser: Perish the thought of flocks of open-armed economists! No, we are not looking to come up with a breakthrough in economic theory. Rather we are
continuously searching for a practical and easier way
to help people make more effective decisions. We
have only limited resources. The best we can do is help
find a way to use them more wisely.

This subject of wise decision making raises a third,
even more intriguing application for computers. I
believe the computer can help us encode the wisdom
of the world and make it easily available to all who
desire to draw upon it.

Brannan: Many ideas are bundled up into this last statement. I
think it would be helpful to explain them one by one.

Gresser: Okay. The first step is to make the link between
integrity and wisdom. We have characterized integrity
as a principle of nature that can be understood and
cultivated through diligent practice. You remember
the example of the unicelled creature surrounded
by a toxic field—how this little thing would take practical steps to hold onto its sense of connectiveness,
coherence, wholeness and vitality—its integrity. This
decision to hold integrity will be a "wise" decision. The
path of wisdom and the path of integrity are the same.
If integrity is a skill, then wisdom also is a trainable
skill.

Let us discuss how the computer can encode wisdom
and make it available to us whenever we are in greatest need of it. In our discussion today we have touched
on many key words—integrity, the five core values,
The Five Rings, PIPs, *lōgōs*, *gravitas*, the principles of
matching/mismatching, containment and abun-
dance, and so forth. Based on all these key words and
concepts, we can construct an integrity index, and
with this index we can build a data base incorporat-
ing all the insights pertinent to each category.

But now something interesting happens. First, we have a way to record our own best thoughts, insights and discoveries. This is not trivial, Tod. If one looks around today at all the problems, one might easily conclude that there is little wisdom in the world. But I do not believe this is true. There is much wisdom. I have found the day laborer, the taxi driver, the poor and disenfranchised have as much wisdom in their hearts and souls as the powerful, the rich and the well-educated—indeed often more because they are less encumbered—but most people, irrespective of class or status or education, do not know how to find their own wisdom. The computer can help train and refine the skill.

This indexing system now provides an easy means for a company, firm, or foundation to take stock of everything that is good and noble in its history, then encode these principles for its management and employees in concrete cases, animating them perhaps by multimedia techniques so their "lessons" can be absorbed in interesting and enjoyable ways. By means of this "wisdom audit" an organization can revive its vision, recreate itself and gain a strong competitive edge.

Stretching the applications of indexing even further, we now have a way to scan all the great works of literature and art (even music) and to find there the essential insights from the viewpoint of integrity. We can store these insights within the computer's memory—the wisdom database—so that players anywhere can instantly obtain coaching on demand on any issue.

Brannan: It might be entertaining to show how Shakespeare, by this method, can become your personal coach.

Gresser: Fair enough. Shakespeare was not only a great poet and playwright. He also looked deeply into the nature of things. Suppose you want some help in dropping assumptions or expectations, or in developing your vigilance in dealing with the Trolls, or in becoming more aware of your own vulnerabilities. You "click" upon any of these headings and instantly a picture of Shakespeare appears. (Actually the program can be designed so that either you "click" or Shakespeare contacts you—E-Mail from Shakespeare!) Then in his own words (given the advances in multimedia it will require little effort to design software so that a verisimilitude of Shakespeare actually speaks to you) the master counsels you through his alter ego, Banquo in *Macbeth*:

> *"But 'tis strange:*
> *And oftentimes, to win us to our harm,*
> *The instruments of darkness tell us truths,*
> *Win us with honest trifles, to betray's*
> *In deepest consequence."*

We are playthings, Shakespeare is warning us. There are truly baleful forces in the world and we ignore them at our peril. Assume nothing!

If we can extract the deepest insights from Shakespeare, we can do the same with Goethe, the Bible, the Baghavad Gita, Leonardo da Vinci, Lincoln, Gandhi, and all the great figures of history, living and dead, and from literature, the epic heroes, the wisest people, and they can all, by means of the computer, become our friends and teachers! If we had **THE WISDOM GENOME** the financial means we could construct for every country its Wisdom Genome—the core of its contribution of wisdom to humanity—to be updated continuously and made available, as a birthright, for everyone.

Brannan: What role do you see the Worldwide Web, the Internet, and communications networks of the future playing in this process?

Gresser: Although, Tod, you probably have much better
                  insights on this question than I, perhaps I can sum-
                  marize some important observations we have made
                  to date training people in The Five Rings via elec-
                  tronic networks.

                  We are building The Logos Network—a community
                  of people around the world who are dedicated to
                  developing integrity through *lōgōs*. Already we have
                  up and running an Electronic Conference/Training
                  Hall called LogosNet which is linked to the Internet.
                  At present the main areas of activity are the East Asian
                  Negotiators' Alliance, the European Negotiators'
                  Alliance, the Environmental Leaders' Roundtable,
                  and The Five Rings Forum. The idea is to include in
                  each of these substantive areas leading specialists as
                  well as players around the world who are involved in
                  international or domestic negotiations, marketing
                  and sales, project management, reengineering, cre-
                  ativity and invention, alternative dispute settlement,
                  and a host of other issues. The Information Super-
                  Highway is ideally suited to launching this experiment
                  in international learning and skill-development along
                  the lines we are contemplating.

Brannan: Before you touch on the substance, it may be useful
                  to address up-front two important concerns many
                  busy people have today about networks. I refer specif-
                  ically to the widespread perception that a network is
                  a form of lonely hearts club, and second, especially
                  for people in business, that to contribute ideas or
                  information to a network—even a private conference
                  group—risks giving away a strategic competitive
                  advantage.

Gresser: These are serious practical considerations. With
                  regard to the first objection, it is true many networks
                  have degenerated into gab groups, and even worse,
                  into opportunities to pander child pornography or
                  violence. The abuse is inherent in the medium. If the

users are degenerate, the network will also be degenerate. But most networks are not this way. In our venture, because everyone who participates will possess a common method, a code of communication and a personal dedication to cultivating integrity, the work of these groups can be focused, effective and creative.

The second objection appears a very real concern for business people. I have a friend, a prominent lawyer and scholar, whom I would like to involve in some way in our efforts. His first reaction was, "I will have to think carefully about what my firm will say. The worse case would be that by participating I might breed legions of competitors!" This is an old way of thinking. Whenever we open our mouth in a seminar or a symposium we are giving away something. The question is what do we get back? Some people will not understand, but others will. They will see that when the goal is integrity, the return is only enhanced for everyone by each new entrant to the Network.

I could make this point more concretely by citing some examples of how a modern community on the general lines of the Taoist model might evolve out of The Lōgōs Network and other allied networks imbued with the same spirit.

The first important observation we have made, quite startling to me as I am still learning about computers, is that it is possible to train hundreds, even thousands of people in an instant. This is because we always work on basics. A player logs on: "Help me with **no assumptions**. I understand the concept," he writes, "but I cannot put it into practice." I or someone else types in a few coaching types, and then click! a hundred other people who are struggling with this same issue can be helped.

On the same lines: Another player is about to enter

a critical stage in a negotiation (Ring 4) and hesitates to grant her opponent the opportunity to say 'no.' "I understand the principle. I read the tutorial in the software program. I have even practiced in low-risk situations. But still it seems unnatural. I'm afraid," she writes. Her inquiry resonates with many others. But then ten people reply, "I didn't believe it either. But here's what I did and look at the results," writes one. "Try this," writes another. "The software doesn't quite make this clear, but if you do it in this way, it is really powerful. I have found that people appreciate not being pushed." So the first player who is struggling with 'no' takes their advice to heart, makes a decision, and takes the action. That's the key, the Act! Perhaps she stumbles. So what? She has a hundred—over a thousand—comrades-in-arms who are rooting for her. She **will** succeed in the end, if she persists.

Deploying the Network for reconnaissance is another use. "I am negotiating a joint venture with the Hung Yueh Petroleum Company in Beijing," logs on an American businessman. "Has anyone developed a PIPs on the decision makers?" Instantly a player in London responds, "This may be helpful to you," and sends him a PIPs in code. The American businessman immediately gains an edge.

The Network could bring help to environmental groups even in the most remote areas of the world, and thereby possibly shift the balance of power in a critical way. Take for example the class action suit recently filed by a group of indigenous people in Ecuador against one of the huge U.S.-headquartered multinational oil companies. The complaint charges that the oil company's wastes are destroying their rain forest habitat, and also are poisoning their drinking water and food supplies. The Five Rings method will provide this group with a new and powerful tool to develop and to coordinate strategies with their U.S. counsel and concerned environmental organizations, conduct reconnaissance, and concentrate all their resources on raising the price (pain) to the oil company of not taking responsible action.

The third insight, which became immediately obvious once we established LogosNet, is that one person's success encourages others to succeed. A player, a venture capitalist, comes to a training workshop. He is trying to persuade a bank in Hong Kong to continue its support to one of his firm's portfolio companies. He uses The Five Rings and "wins" the negotiation. The bank stays in. It is worth a few million dollars to him. With his permission I write up the case (preserving the anonymity of all parties). Everyone on the Network immediately learns of his victory and, more importantly, sees how he concretely worked the system. "If **he** can do it, **I** can do it," each person says to him or herself.

Paying forward is also wonderfully enhanced by the Network. Ten players have wins. Some modest, some great. They log on: "We wish to pay our gains forward, they write, they have brought us much joy. Who knows of cases of great need where we might be of some help?" From across the world instantly come the replies: This player knows victims of an earthquake in Greece. A negotiator in Chile logs on about a family he knows with a child who is deformed because his mother took thalidomide. A group in Brazil appeals for help in its fight to preserve the rain forest. The general counsel of a leading pharmaceutical company writes that his firm is a member of the Make-A-Wish Foundation, that he knows of a child in New Hampshire with an inoperable brain tumor who wants to break the Guinness Book of Records on get-well cards before he dies. The connections are made and countless selfless actions taken, quietly and unobtrusively, falling as the gentle rain from heaven.

Brannan:	What then is the question?
Gresser:	The question is when will the transition begin from this Age of Noise to an Age of Wisdom? It seems we have waited a very long time.

Can a single person change the course of history for ill? It appears so. At least a single individual can pre-cipitate the change. Did not a single madman by a single evil act—the assassination of Gandhi—change irrevocably the course of India's history? What about a single generous act? Why then cannot a single act of kindness, warmth and cheer reverse the course of evil? What about a hundred acts by a hundred peo-ple or who knows how many by what number, of countless unheralded acts of goodness over time? What might be their effects? Where is the threshold that, once breached, could bring a watershed of ben-eficial change?

There is a very interesting movie, *Weapons of the Spirit*, which I recommend strongly to all those who are interested in these matters. It describes life in a small French town in the Pyrenees during World War II. It was a town occupied mainly by Huguenots, which per-haps provides a clue, because these were people inured to struggle and hardship, who throughout their history had dedicated themselves to compas-sionate service. In every other town in the area the Jews had been shipped off to concentration camps, but in this town the Jewish community went on liv-ing a normal life, without going into hiding, raising children, sending them to school, attending to daily chores, and burying the dead. In the center of the town the Gestapo made its headquarters, but for some reason they took no notice of the Jews who were right under their noses.

"We did what we had to do," explained some old men

and women in the town when they were interviewed years later by a Jewish photographer who as a child growing up in the town had himself witnessed it all. There were no plots, no sabotage, no subterfuge. "We did what seemed right and natural at the time, that was all." And the Gestapo, for this brief moment, either failed to see, or would not act.

The producer of *Weapons of the Spirit* described what happened in this town as a "conspiracy of good"—a shaft of light in a dark and gruesome period.

That is our goal: to set in motion such conspiracies of good and see if, together, we can help Fortune turn her Wheel.

Brannan: To where could this ultimately lead?

Gresser: I do not know. I am content to enjoy the mystery of it. My feelings are expressed in this passage by Albert Camus, which responds to your question of where things could lead.

Brannan: What did Camus say?

Gresser: "Great ideas come into the world as gently as doves, perhaps, then, if we listen attentively, we shall hear, amid the uproar of empires and nations, a faint flutter of wings, the gentle stirring of life and hope. Some will say that this hope lies in a nation; others in the men. I believe that it is awakened, revived, nourished by millions of solitary individuals whose deeds and works every day negate frontiers, and the crudest implications of history . . . each and every person, on the foundation of his or her own suffering and joys, builds for all."

GLOSSARY OF KEY TERMS AND CONCEPTS

Act with Integrity	To embody integrity by action. Goethe writes: "It says: 'In the beginning was the word' already I am stopped. It seems absurd. The word does not deserve the highest prize . . . The spirit helps me. Now it is exact. I write: 'In the beginning was the Act.'" Without using words or thoughts see if you can express your integrity to someone else, right now!
Agenda	A technique used to address real problems, our and another player's concerns (baggage) what we want and what happens next. Agenda always "floats" in The Five Rings system meaning that you can use the technique at any stage in a negotiation.
Agent	An agent is a person who acts on behalf of, or in lieu of, a principal.
Ask Your Integrity	To seek guidance from your innermost core. Timing is important and so is auspices: we pay respect to the source. In Japanese the word for "god," *kami,* is written with the Chinese character "to speak" beside "platform" or "dias." To ask your integrity is to initiate a dialogue with your True Self, face-to-face.
Assessor	An assessor is a person with superior analytical abilities.
Assumptions	The word "ass-u-me" tells it all. Assumptions invariably make an ass of you and me. The goal is to test all important assumptions.
Attack Integrity	To assault another's integrity with the intention of severing the connection.
Blocker	A blocker is a player who guards the interests of the key decision makers.
Brush	Interrogatory questions—'who', 'when', 'where', 'why', 'how',—are powerful techniques to open our and another player's discovery process.

Budget	Negotiating budget includes time with a value of 1, effort with a value of 2, money (meaning percentage of resources actually committed) with a value of 3, and creative emotion (vitality) with a value of 4. The Artful Navigator manages all four elements of budget efficiently, paying special attention to safeguarding creative vitality (emotion), the most precious asset.
Catalyst	A catalyst is a player who brings energy and sparkle to his (her) comrades and inspires change.
Catastrophe	Act of panic resulting from the perception (usually invalid) of extreme need.
Checkpoint	Whenever you reach an "understanding" in a negotiation or discover something important, you can anchor this perception with the Checkpoint. The Checkpoint simply repeats and reflects back (usually three times or more) the perception. Most people wear 'masks.' (The word 'person' originally meant 'mask.') They have become so accustomed to the mask they can no longer see the face. The Checkpoint helps you see the face behind the mask.
Compromise Integrity	To prostitute or to give up integrity for something of lesser value.
Containment	The ability to hold thoughts and emotions coherently together especially under duress.
Contaminate Integrity	Refers to how one person's lapse of integrity can infect and undermine another's.
Critical Parent	A move designed to make you feel like an angry, helpless and accommodating child. A recent example of Critical Parent is the Japanese government's blaming American consumers for their "dirty habits" as an explanation of why seatbelts provided by Japanese companies were defective in the United States. The best antidote to Critical Parent is simply to stay present and light, and keep your sense of fun and play.
Cultivate Integrity	Refers to the process by which we gradually build the ves

sel of character that allows us to navigate productively in the world.

Decision Maker(s)	Key people who are in a position to make what you want happen.
Dragon	"Dragon" comes from the Greek word "dukein" meaning "to see." There is a famous Buddhist saying, "When the universe roars, only the heavenly dragon watches calmly and with pure delight." The world can be topsy-turvey, but your dragon energy observes, seeing all, understanding all, content in its power.
	The dragon is the child of the four elements: air, water, earth, fire. She lives in pools, in the bowels of the earth, in the shadows of caves, in the mists. She is your reticulated power.
	When you connect to your integrity, the power uncoils and then the dragon, in all its glory, steps forth.
Dumping	Impulsively to divulge information.
Expectations	An expectation is an assumption with an ego complex (see Assumptions). Unruly expectations get us into even more trouble than assumptions. The rule is the same: drop all expectations and become alive!
Fall Out of Integrity	To lose your line (connection) to the universe.
"Field Effect"	A change in one person's consciousness as the result of changes in another's consciousness or in the physical environment.
Follow Your Integrity	The specific act of being guided by integrity as well as the pursuit of its life-path.
Gather Integrity	To collect one's scattered consciousness by becoming aware and present.
Goal	An action or quality of behavior or character that advances

your mission. You must focus on goals you can manage well, i.e., your own action/behavior, not illusory goals such as results or other people's actions or behavior that you cannot manage.

Gravitas	The condition of wakefulness, steadiness and equanimity derived from disciplined practice of presence.
Hold Integrity	To maintain integrity—connectedness, coherence, whole ness, and vitality— under stress or in the face of pain.
IBUs	A measure of your complete budget consisting of time, energy, financial reserves and creative vitality (emotion).
Integrity	Sense of connectedness, coherence, wholeness, and vitality.
Kaizen	Japanese term for continuous improvement. Originally used in engineering systems, adapted and broadened here as a fundamental principle of effective action.
Know Your Integrity	To feel whole and alive, connected and coherent, and will ing to let your spirit go forth into the world and be of use.
Listen to Integrity	We listen to our integrity not only with our ears, but also with our eyes, our stomachs—with our whole body and mind. It is different from ordinary listening—quieter, more profound. And what we listen for is also different. Our integrity may express itself not only in words or thoughts, but also in images, dreams, or events in the external world. When we listen to our integrity in this way we open ourselves to the signal wherever it appears.
Lōgōs	In Greek, Lōgōs meant both the spoken word and the pervading principle of reason. The Stoics saw *lōgōs* as the ordering principle of the universe. Like the Chinese Tao, the wise person, they believed, would aim to live in harmony with it. In the prologue of the Gospel according to John, the *lōgōs* is the Divine Word, a self-communicating divine presence that exists with God and is uniquely manifest in Jesus Christ.
Loss	Any move away from integrity.

'Maybe'   An equivocal limbo-state between 'yes' and 'no'. A 'maybe'
                   moves an untrained negotiator into precarious waters
                   because it defers an effective decision.

Mission and   The negotiator's navigational compass, the basic discov
Purpose   ery tool and means to allocate scarce resources of time,
                   effort, money, and creative emotion. "Mission" is the over-
                   all direction; "purpose" captures in a single word or phrase
                   the intention of an enterprise.

Muses   In Greek mythology the Muses were daughters of
                   Mnemosyne (Memory) and Zeus—the fruits, it is said, of
                   nine nights of love-making. They presided over thought
                   in all its forms: eloquence, persuasion, knowledge, history,
                   mathematics, and astronomy. Hesiod claimed that they
                   accompanied kings and inspired them with the persuasive
                   words necessary to settle quarrels and reestablish peace,
                   and gave to kings the gentleness that made them dear to
                   their subjects.

Navigate   To move your cause forward by intelligent and wise deci-
                   sion making, character, and effective negotiation. "Navi-
                   gation" is the process of doing so.

Need   Field dependence. Need says, "If I don't have it, I will surely
                   die." Examples of what we really need: O_2, water, food,
                   sleep, shelter—not much else.

Negative   The principle of Negative Multiplier refers to a falling out
Multiplier   of integrity in one place that impairs integrity in another,
                   and with compound interest. In the history of kings,
                   Achilles, King Lear, Macbeth and Othello, the single flaw
                   of hubris -overweening pride—could so eat away at char-
                   acter that the whole person was destroyed. It is the same
                   with organizations, communities, even nations. When
                   integrity is torn, troubles come not singly but in troops.

Negotiate   "To succeed in getting over or across, or up and down (as
                   a hill), or through (as an obstacle)," Webster's 3d Inter-
                   national Dictionary.

'No'   A signalling device. The trained negotiator welcomes a 'no' because he/she understands it enables an effective decision.

Pain   The first noble truth in Buddhism, the universal condition. Everyone alive has pain in one form or another.

Pain/Need Ratio   The relationship between pain and need. The most effective negotiators are able to become present to their pain or "hold integrity" in the face of pain and thereby find their power.

Pay Forward   To celebrate a win and then pass its joy and other benefits onward to another person without seeking any monetary compensation or other recompense.

Pendulum   A technique and indicator of where to position one's self emotionally in a negotiation. When another player is very positive, the pendulum suggests we stand positive, but slightly less positive; when another player is negative, the pendulum counsels that we place ourselves in a slightly more negative position to allow the other player space to exercise his/her right to say 'no'.

PIPs   Player Integrity Profiles—a key tool in assessing the "source code" of character from the perspective of integrity.

Positive Multiplier   As the number of beneficial deeds increases and their rate accelerates, much like bombarded neutrons in a nuclear chain reaction, a critical mass is reached. Then an explosion can occur of such human warmth, kindness, generosity and cheer that the world might never recover from it.

Practice Integrity   The conscious and disciplined process of cultivating integrity, particularly by the accumulation of "cases" from the field of action. The Five Rings, the Weekly, Action and Discovery Logs in combination with the tutorial on "How to Practice" constitute a complete system for the cultivation and practice of integrity.

Presentation   The act of helping another player discover how his/her pain can be relieved and principal problems addressed.

	In The Five Rings the most effective presentations are made to the key decision maker(s).
Rebuild Integrity	Conscious work to strengthen the container or foundation, i.e., character.
Reclaim (Restore) Integrity	Refers to the process of returning to the path of integrity.
Reverse	The act of turning the tables on an opponent or situation. For example, the move of pausing, struggling, and then responding to a question with a countervailing question, usually an interrogatory question. As you practice integrity, you learn the art of reversing "reverses" of fortune.
Scalpel	Verb-led questions such as 'are', 'do', 'should', 'can', 'will', 'may'. The Scalpel is a risky way for an untrained negotiator to initiate a dialogue.
Scouts	Scouts are players with a superior ability to gather information and to perform reconnaissance.
Spilling	Impulsively breaking the container and leaking the emotions.
Surrender Integrity	A general reference to relinquishing integrity.
Trainability	The ability to adjust instantly in any situation resulting from an openness and curiosity to learn from error and failure.
Trolls	Trolls (Trollensis Horribilis) are unpleasant, smelly creatures usually found living under bridges (concrete and spiritual) in troops. As creatures of the shadow world, Trolls will attack and seek to undermine your integrity. Advanced players learn how to tap Troll energy for constructive purposes.
Undermine Integrity	An assault upon integrity either by direct or surreptitious means with the intention of disturbing the very foundation.

The Will | The Will is the capacity of complex living things to choose freely, often in unprogrammed and unpredictable ways, and to take responsibility for their actions. If you are the Captain, the Will is the means by which you direct your ship. It is the way you pilot your course and set the sails to take advantage of the winds and currents. The Will is a "metaforce" to be distinguished from "will power," which implies simply brute force.

Win | Any step, however modest, that advances a valid mission.

BIBLIOGRAPHY

The following books have been helpful to me and may be useful to readers who wish to explore further some of the themes in this book.

CLASSICS

MARCUS AURELIUS. *Meditations* (translated by Maxwell Stanforth, 1964)

THE BIBLE. Old and New Testaments

CHARLES DICKENS. *A Christmas Carol* (Simon and Schuster, 1939), *Hard Times* (Penguin Books)

RALPH WALDO EMERSON. Essay on Compensation in *The Portable Emerson*, Viking paperback, 1946

GOETHE. *Faust* (translated by Walter Kaufmann, 1961)

HEKIGANROKU . *Blue Cliff Record* (translated by Kōun Yamada and Robert Aitken)

HERAKLEITOS. *Herakleitos and Diogones* (translated by Guy Davenport, 1983)

HOMER. *Iliad and Odyssey* (translated by Robert Fitzgerald)

VICTOR HUGO. *Les Miserables* (translated by Norman Denney, 1976)

I CHING. *Book of Changes* (translated by Hellmut Wilhelm, 1950)

NIKOS KAZANTZIKAS. *Zorba the Greek* (translated by Carl Wildman, 1952)

MASTERS OF HUAINAN. *The Art of Politics* (Translated by Thomas Cleary (Shambhala), 1961)

MUMONKAN. *Gateless Gate* (translated by Kōun Yamada)

MUSASHI MIYAMOTO. *The Book of Five Rings* (translated by Victor Harris, 1974)

PLATO. *The Phaedrus* (translated by Walter Hamilton, Penguin Books, 1973)

SHAKESPEARE . *Henry V, MacBeth, King Lear, Othello, Richard III, Julius Caesar, The Merchant of Venice, Hamlet*

SHŌYŌROKU . *Book of Serenity* (translated by Kōun Yamada and Robert Aitken)

MU SOENG SUNIM. *Heart Sutra* (1991)

SUN TZU. *The Art of War* (translated by Lionel Giles, 1988)

TAO TE CHING. *The Way of Subtle Virtues* (translated by John C. H. Wu, 1961)

MARK TWAIN. *The Unabridged Mark Twain* (Running Press, 1976)

CONTEMPORARY

PETER ACKROYD. *Dickens* (1990)

ROBERT AITKEN. *Taking the Path of Zen* (1982)

JOHN BEEBE. *Integrity in Depth* (1992)

RICHARD CARSON. *Taming Your Gremlin* (Harper Perennial, 1983)

STEVEN R. COVEY. *The 7 Habits of Highly Effective People* (1990)

J. W. DUNNE. *An Experiment With Time* (1927)

ROGER FISHER/WILLIAM URY. *Getting to Yes* (1981)

VICTOR FRANKL. *Man's Search for Meaning* (Copyright 1984)

HOWARD GARDNER. *Creating Minds* (1993)

LAURIE GARRETT. *The Coming Plague* (1994)

ELMER AND ALYCE GREEN. *Beyond Biofeedback* (Knoll Publishing Company, 1977)

WILLIS HARMAN AND HOWARD RHEINGOLD *Higher Creativity,* Liberating the Unconscious for Breakthrough Insights (1984)

ANDREW KILPATRICK. *Of Permanent Value—The Story of Warren Buffett* (1994)

ARTHUR KOESTLER. *The Act of Creation* (1964)

JACQUES LUSSEYRAN. *And There Was Light* (Parabola Books, 1991)

ALAN MOOREHEAD. *The Fatal Impact* (1966)

MICHAEL RAY AND ROCHELLE MEYERS. *Creativity in Business* (1986)

DONALD T. PHILLIPS. *Lincoln on Leadership* (1992)

HOWARD RHEINGOLD. *The Virtual Community* (1993)

RAINER MARIA RILKE. *Selected Poetry* (Edited and Translated by Steven Mitchell (1980)

ROBERT SCOTT ROOT-BERNSTEIN. *Discovering* (1989)

LAWRENCE SUSSKIND/JEFFREY CRUIKSHANK. *Breaking the Impasse* (1987)

JOHN TARRANT. *The Light Inside The Dark* (1996)

SAM WALTON. *Sam Walton Made In America*, 1992

Those readers particularly interested in the Japanese negotiating code can refer to:

THOMAS CLEARY. *The Japanese Art of War* (1991)

TAKEO DOI. *The Anatomy of Independence* (Amae no Kōzō) (1971)

MICHIHIRO MATSUMOTO. *The Unspoken Way* (1988)

TREVOR LEGGETT. *Zen in the Ways* (1978)

TAKIE SUGIYAMA LEBRA. *Japanese Patterns of Behavior* (1976)

JULIAN GRESSER. *Breaking the Japanese Negotiating Code: What European and American Managers Must Do to Win* (European Management Journal Vol. 10 No. 3 September 1992)

JULIAN GRESSER. *Understanding the Japanese Negotiating Code: The Virtual Dōjō and Other Critical Capabilities for the Late 1990s* (Presented at the Southwestern Legal Foundation Symposium on Private Investments Abroad June 20-21, 1995)

For an appreciation of Japan's contributions to the field of integrity in action, the reader can refer to:

PAUL REPS. *Zen Flesh, Zen Bones* (1961)

Index

Ability to Attend   100; 118; 120; 121
Abyss   58;
Action Log   126; 128; 129; 152;
Aeschylus   38;
Agamemnon   38;
Age of Wisdom   145;
Age of Noise   145;
Agenda   48; 50; 51; 53; 73; 91; 126; 147;
Agents   41; 43; 44; 45; 147
Aristos   8;
Ask Your Integrity   105; 147;
Arrogance, Vanity and Greed (see also
   PIPs)   63; 94; 99; 101; 104; 107; 116;
   120; 121;
Artful Navigator, The   XII; 148; 160;
Baghavad Gita   140;
Basho   1;
Beauty   XVI; 34; 35; 67; 130; 133; 136;
Biofeedback   9;
Black Curtain (Kuromaku)   41;
Blockers   44; 45; 48; 86; 147;
Breyer, Steven - Supreme Court Justice
   40;
Brush, The   77; 82; 147;
Budget   20; 27; 29; 32; 38; 40; 44; 48;
   49; 50; 51; 55; 56; 78; 79; 126; 148;
Building the container   58; 59; 63; 90;
Camus, Albert   146;
Captain Cook   68;
Chaos   7; 8; 15; 18; 25; 58; 59; 91; 125;
   132;
Character   X; 7; 8; 12; 45; 56; 96; 97;
   99; 103; 135; 149; 151; 152; 153;
Checkpoint   91; 92; 93; 147;
Chi (qi)   118;
China   10; 12; 51; 58; 96; 97; 105; 112;
   118; 147;
Chopra,   Deepak9;
Churchill, Sir Winston   45; 63;
Coherence   8; 26; 113;
Coleridge, Samuel Taylor   66;
Connectors   49; 63; 65; 85; 107;
Consciousness   9; 16; 29; 56; 61; 65; 91;
   104; 106; 109; 124; 149;
Consensus Trance   68; 69;
Conspiracy of Good   146;
Continuity as Power   129;
Creative Reverie   30; 36; 51; 83; 88; 104;

106; 128; 130; 137; 142; 148; 150;
Creativity   18; 29; 30; 50; 64; 78; 80; 81;
   104; 114; 115; 117; 137; 141;
Crisis (weiji)   59; 65;
Curiosity   40; 76; 90;
Dante   106;
Decision Makers   IX; 38; 39; 40; 43; 44;
   48; 49; 50; 58; 126; 138; 149;
Default Moves   35; 36; 43; 48; 53; 55;
Dickens, Charles   114;
Digital SuperHighway   48; 141;
Discovery Questions   77; 96;
Discovery   VIII; IX: XI: XII; 43; 64; 67;
   72; 74; 76; 77; 78; 81; 83; 85; 88; 90;
   91; 96; 112; 113; 114; 116; 118; 119;
   120; 124; 126; 130; 136; 148; 151; 152;
Dragon in the Clouds   41; 45;
Each moment has equal dignity   63;
Earn what you want (See also the Five
   Core Values)   14; 23;
Ease116;
East Asia Negotiators' Alliance   55;
Embrace the 'no' (See also the Five Core
   Values)   15; 16; 99;
Emerson, Ralph Waldo   13;
Emotions   39; 40; 45; 48; 51; 62; 65; 88;
   90; 91; 94; 103; 116; 121; 152; 153;
Environmental Leaders Network   141;
Entrope   IX; X; 8;
Equal Dignity   18;
Eternal Present   18;
Ethics   IX; 12;
European Negotiators' Alliance   141;
"Fall Off"   136;
Fatal Impact, The   68;
Faust   91;
Fear   9; 17; 45; 46; 62; 63; 64; 66; 67; 74;
   75; 99; 116;
Few needs (See also the Five Core Val-
   ues)   15;
Five (5)   126;
Five Core Values, The   13; 30; 36; 51;
   52; 56; 68; 91; 138;
Five Rings, The   XI; XIV; 17; 30; 35; 56;
   58; 79; 91; 96; 104; 108; 112; 137; 138;
   141; 143; 144; 147; 152; 153; 160;
Focus (see also PIPs)   26; 31; 32; 35; 46;
   49; 63; 90; 93; 95; 100; 102; 109; 113;

119; 150;
Fortune   146;
Four (4)   91;
Frankl, Victor   34;
Gandhi, Mahatma   140; 145;
Getz Brothers   37; 132;
Goethe, Johann Wolfgang von   140; 147;
Gospel of John   105; 150;
Grandiosity   116; 121;
Gravitas   7; 49; 63; 66; 75; 100; 102; 103; 104; 118; 121; 138; 150;
Greece   XI; 7; 8; 58; 96; 104; 136; 144; 151;
Hakuin   84;
Heart/Mind   60; 69; 73; 74; 75; 76; 90; 94; 95; 130; 150
Herakleitos   7;
Hierarchy of Missions   27;
Honne   93;
Hold Integrity   83; 87; 97; 124; 129; 138; 150; 152;
Homeostasis   9;
How to See   74;
Huguenots   145;
Humility   55;
I Ching   7; 55;
Inferno   106;
Information SuperHighway   48; 141;
Integrity   IX; XI; XII; XIV; 2; 8; 9; 10; 12; 13; 14; 17; 25; 26; 28; 29; 30; 31; 35; 36; 38; 47; 49; 52; 54; 55; 56; 57; 58; 62; 63; 66; 67; 71; 73; 82; 83; 84; 90; 91; 96; 97; 99; 100; 107; 108; 109; 114; 116; 118; 119; 120 125; 128; 129; 130; 132; 133; 134; 135; 136; 138; 139; 141; 142; 147; 148; 149; 150; 151; 152; 153; 157;
Integrity Budget Units (IBUs)   28; 29; 32; 137;
Internet   XII; XIV; 140; 141; 160;
Intuition   94; 104; 106;
Intuition in Action Forum   126; 128; 129; 152;
Japan   25; 36; 41; 42; 44; 45; 74;
Japanese Negotiating Code   VIII; IX; X; 2; 31; 38; 46; 47; 5`; 69; 70; 65; 91; 95; 109; 147;
Kaizen   112; 150;
Keats   77;
Kurosawa, Akira   75;

Law of Compensation   104;
Leadership   8; 53;
Leonardo da Vinci   XII; 68; 140;
"Life Pie"   30; 137;
Lincoln, Abraham   83; 140;
Listening   94; 95
Logos   XV; 138; 141; 150;
Logos Networks Corporation   24; 27; 104; 105; 131; 141; 142;
Logos Net141; 144; 160;
Macbeth   140;
Man's Search for Meaning   34;
Mandate of Heaven   10;
Mind   60; 69; 73; 74; 75; 76; 90; 94; 95; 130; 150;
Mission and Purpose   14; 23; 24; 25; 27; 30; 32; 36; 38; 39; 44; 45; 46; 47; 48; 51; 55; 56; 72; 73; 78; 81; 88; 108; 109; 112; 113; 115; 126; 129; 132; 133; 150; 151;
Mnemosyne (Memory)   136;
Modesty   104; 129; 130; 135;
Moorehead, Alan   68;

Morality   135;
Muses   115; 136; 151;
Nature   35; 58; 128; 135; 138;
Navigation   VIII; IX; X; XI; XIV; 2; 44; 132; 151;
Need   15; 16; 17; 18; 35; 53; 54; 65; 71; 73; 77; 84; 90; 92; 95; 99; 103; 109; 116; 118; 121; 144; 151; 152;
Negative Capability   64; 65;
Negative Halucination   64; 65;
Negotiation   X; 7; 8; 13; 15; 26; 28; 31; 32; 35; 37; 38; 43; 44; 46; 48; 49; 50; 53; 54; 55; 58; 65; 67; 73; 76; 79; 81; 85; 86; 87; 91; 94; 95; 104; 112; 113; 115; 117; 119; 128; 132; 141; 143; 144; 147; 148; 151;
No Dumping   44;
No   17; 39; 52; 53; 54; 55; 56; 77; 85; 88; 90; 92; 101; 143; 151; 152;
No Assumptions/No Expectations (See also the Five Core Values)   14; 16; 20; 40; 67; 70; 71; 73; 74; 75; 76; 91; 99; 100; 142; 147;
No Assumptions/No Expectations (see also PIPs)   106;
No Spilling   44; 87;
Not-Okay-on-Purpose   83; 84; 85;

Note taking   91; 93; 94;
Nurturing   82; 83; 87; 100; 104;
Odysseus   8; 66; 83;
One (1)   92;
Pain   38; 39; 40; 41; 44; 48; 49; 50; 51;
    52; 53; 56; 78; 79; 83; 101; 109; 125;
    126; 129; 132; 144; 152;
Pain/Need Ratio   99; 101; 102; 152;
Pandemonium   58;
Parry   85;
Pay Forward   108; 118; 120; 126; 129;
    133; 144; 152;
Pendulum, The   88; 90; 152;
PIPs (Player Integrity Profiles)   96; 97;
    101; 102; 103; 104; 138; 143; 152;
Practice Everything With Everything
    130;
Presence   18; 36; 49; 51; 52; 53; 58; 59;
    63; 66; 74; 85; 95; 96; 102; 126; 129;
    132; 133;
Presentation   43; 44; 48; 49; 50; 51; 52;
    53; 54; 86; 95; 126; 152;
Principle of Matching/Mismatching,
    The (see also PIPs)   104;
Qi Gong   12;
Reconnaissance   38; 41; 06; 143; 144;
Reverse, The   85; 90; 153;
Rilke, Rainer Maria   125;
Ronin   76;
Samurai   75; 76;
Saper vedere   68;
Scalpel, The   77; 78; 153;
Scouts   41; 43; 44; 45; 153;
See the world as it is   118; 121;

Shakespeare   XII; 58; 64; 139;
Shin (Heart/Mind)   94; 95;
Siegel, Bernie   9;
Silence   4; 65; 70; 85; 87; 91; 96;
Spies   42; 44;
Sweden   46; 47;
T. E. Lawrence   131;
Tao   105; 135; 142; 150;
"Te"   10;
Ten (10)   10;
The Logos Network   24; 27; 104; 105;
    131; 141; 142;
Three (3)   91;
Trainability   7; 31; 94; 97; 103; 125; 129;
Trolls   45; 58; 117; 121; 140; 153;
Truth   38;
Vanity   45; 66; 116; 119; 121;
Vision   21; 105; 132;
Vitality   8; (see also Budget)
Weapons of the Spirit   145;
Weekly Log, The   112; 113; 115; 125;
    126; 129; 152;
Wheel of Fortune, The   V; 124; 146;
Will, The   45; 46; 66; 118; 120; 121;
    154;
"Win-Win" Negotiations   X; XI; 109;
Wisdom   7; 17; 38; 105; 109; 138; 139;
    140;
Wisdom Audit   139;
Wisdom Genome   140;
Wonder   40;
Yes   31; 39; 54; 78; 151;
Zuigan   67; 100;

Continuing Your Practice

There are many ways you can continue to practice. You will be most welcome in any of the special workshops we have organized in collaboration with leading experts around the world. These include seminars on "Artful International Negotiation," "Understanding the Japanese Negotiating Code," "Effective Environmental Advocacy," "Integrity and Intuition in Action," and "Turning Your Best Ideas Into Practice." If attending workshops is not your thing, The Artful Navigator™ (version 1.1) is also available as a Virtual Executive Coach for those who will find personalized interactive training helpful.

We have also organized a unique Electronic Meeting/Training Hall, LogosNet™, with access to the Internet where you can meet other players around the world, test out your ideas, and hone your skills. LogosNet™ now includes the following conference groups: The International Negotiators' Alliance (including The East Asia Negotiators' Alliance and The European Negotiators' Alliance), The Environmental Leaders' Roundtable, and The Five Rings™ Forum. The idea is to make the practice easy, interesting and fun, and to open as many doors into the Garden as possible, so that you can follow whatever path catches your fancy and explore it as deeply as you wish.

Purchasing Information

The Artful Navigator™ is now available in two forms: a single-user version ($495.00) and a multi-user version ($795.00). To order other copies of *Piloting Through Chaos* , The Artful Navigator™, for further information on our seminars, LogosNet™, or other online products and services, please contact us either by fax (1/510/527-7970), telephone (1/510-527-7970), online (Sales@LogosNet.com) or mail (Logos Networks Corporation, P. O. Box 720, Sausalito, CA 94965). Book shipping details are as follows: Continental U.S.-$2.00 for book rate for first book, $0.75 for each additional book; for Europe-$13.00 surface, call for other options; software shipping (including *Piloting Through Chaos*) Continental U.S. - UPS ground five days-$6.00, two-day UPS, $14.00; Europe - airmail five day, $14.00; call for other options. Payments can be made either by check or Visa card.